Higher

Computing

2001 Exam

2002 Exam

2003 Exam

2004 Exam

2005 Exam – Old Arrangements

2005 SQP – New Arrangements

2005 Exam – New Arrangements

Leckie ×Leckie

First exam published in 2001.

Published by Leckie & Leckie, 8 Whitehill Terrace, St. Andrews, Scotland KY16 8RN tel: 01334 475656 fax: 01334 477392 enquiries@leckieandleckie.co.uk www.leckieandleckie.co.uk

ISBN 1-84372-338-7

A CIP Catalogue record for this book is available from the British Library.

Printed in Scotland by Scotprint.

Leckie & Leckie is a division of Granada Learning Limited, part of ITV plc.

Acknowledgements

Leckie & Leckie is grateful to the copyright holders, as credited at the back of the book, for permission to use their material. Every effort has been made to trace the copyright holders and to obtain their permission for the use of copyright material. Leckie & Leckie will gladly receive information enabling them to rectify any error or omission in subsequent editions.

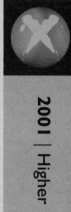

[BLANK PAGE]

X017/301

NATIONAL QUALIFICATIONS 2001	TUESDAY, 5 JUNE 1.00 PM – 3.30 PM	COMPUTING HIGHER

Attempt **all** questions in Section I.

Attempt **four** questions in Section II

Question 13 and Question 14
and **either** Question 15 **or** Question 16
and **either** Question 17 **or** Question 18

Attempt **one** sub-section of Section III.

Part A	Artificial Intelligence	Page 12	Questions 19 to 22
Part B	Computer Networking	Page 15	Questions 23 to 26
Part C	Computer Programming	Page 18	Questions 27 to 30
Part D	Multimedia Technology	Page 22	Questions 31 to 34

For the sub-section chosen, attempt **three** questions.

The **first two** questions and **either** the third question **or** the fourth question.

Read all questions carefully.

Do not write on the question paper.

Write as neatly as possible.

SCOTTISH
QUALIFICATIONS
AUTHORITY

SECTION I

Attempt all questions in this section

Marks

1. A desktop computer is connected to a local-area network.

    (a) Name and draw a labelled diagram of **one** network topology which could be used for the local-area network.   1

    (b) What specific hardware must be present in a computer in order for it to be connected to this network?   1

2. Buffers and spoolers can be used to increase system performance.

    (a) Describe how a buffer will increase system performance.   1

    (b) Describe **one** situation in which a spooler would be used in preference to a buffer.   1

3. Describe **two** different methods you could use to find out whether a graphic was created using a bit-mapped graphics package or a vector graphics package.   2

4. A scanned image measures 3 inches by 4 inches. It was scanned at 600 dpi in 256 colours.

    (a) Calculate the storage requirements for the scanned image in megabytes. Show all your working.   2

    (b) Name **one** storage device which could be used to store the image and give **one** reason for your choice.   2

5. (a) In computer systems, integers are stored using *two's complement representation*. What would be the range of integers which could be stored in **one** byte if two's complement representation was used?   1

    (b) In computer systems, large numbers are stored using *floating point representation*. State the effect of **increasing** the number of bits used to store:

       (i) the mantissa;

       (ii) the exponent.   2

6. Give **one** reason why a computer is often described as a "two-state machine".   1

7. How is memory organised so that data can be stored and retrieved by the processor?   1

Marks

SECTION I (continued)

8. A list of medals won at the Olympic Games is stored in a computer. For each medal, details of the event, name and country of the winner are stored. A program was designed to work out how many medals overall each country won.

   (a) Which **one** of the following algorithms would be needed in this program?
   - (i) Finding maximum
   - (ii) Finding minimum
   - (iii) Counting occurrences
   - (iv) Linear search 1

   (b) Name **two** guides which should be produced during the documentation stage of the software development process. 1

   (c) Give **one** advantage to the software house of distributing these guides on CD ROM. 1

9. The first two stages of the software development process are *analysis* and *design*.

   (a) State the purpose of each of these stages. 2

   (b) What is meant by the term *iterative* during the software development process? 1

10. (a) Give **one** reason why it is important for programmers to ensure that their programs are readable. 1

    (b) Describe **two** different techniques used by programmers to ensure that their programs are readable. 2

11. Describe the purpose of each of the following in a software development environment:
    - (i) editor;
    - (ii) translator;
    - (iii) error tracing tool. 3

12. (a) Some software development environments support *local variables* as well as *global variables*.
    - (i) State what is meant by a "local variable".
    - (ii) Describe how the use of local variables assists with modularity. 2

    (b) State **one** method of storing a list of 100 names input from a keyboard within a program. 1

    (30)

[END OF SECTION I]

SECTION II

Attempt FOUR questions in this section *Marks*

Question 13 and Question 14
and either Question 15 or Question 16
and either Question 17 or Question 18

13. A small company with 200 customers wants to purchase new computers. The IT Manager has noticed two adverts in a computer catalogue.

Pegasus ZX	Hercules EN
333 MHz Processor	366 MHz Processor
64 Mb RAM	64 Mb RAM
2 USB Interfaces	Serial and Parallel Interfaces
4 Gb Hard Disk Drive	10 Gb Hard Disk Drive
24 × CD ROM Drive	40 × CD ROM Drive

(a) (i) Give **two** reasons why *interfaces* are required to connect peripheral devices to the computer.

   (ii) State why there is a need for standardisation of interfaces.

   (iii) In addition to the interface, what addition to the standard operating system will be required so that the CD ROM drive will operate in these computer systems? **4**

(b) The IT Manager believes that the Hercules EN will be the faster computer as it has a 366 MHz processor compared to the 333 MHz Pegasus ZX.

   Suggest **two** reasons why he may be incorrect. **2**

(c) Both systems have 64 Mb of RAM organised as 32-bit words. What is the minimum possible width of the address bus in these systems? Justify your answer. **2**

(d) Since the company may have to store sensitive data about their customers, describe **two** conditions which the company must satisfy in order to protect their customers. **2**

Marks

SECTION II (continued)

14. A program requires the user to input the name of the country where they live. The program is able to accept any one of 157 different country names.

Here are three possible means of entering this information in a graphical user interface.

The user types a name into the box.

The user picks one of the names from the scrolling pop-up menu.

The user can type a name or select from the scrollable list. If the user types, the list automatically scrolls to the closest match in the list. The user can still select from the list at any time.

(a) Describe each of these interfaces in terms of:
   - ease of data entry
   - validity of data entry.   3

(b) If you were the designer of such a program, which **two** questions would you ask to decide which one of these interfaces to specify?   2

(c) Describe how you could test which one of these interfaces was most suitable for this particular purpose.   2

(d) This software will have to be maintained when the name of a country changes. How would the change of a country's name affect the maintenance requirement for each of the three interfaces?   3

[Turn over

Marks

SECTION II (continued)

Attempt either Question 15 or Question 16

15. A video firm creates and edits digital videos using their company's computer system.

    (*a*) Name **three** hardware features that the firm's **computer** must have in order to cope with this task. Give a reason for each of your choices.   **3**

    (*b*) The video company also uses digital cameras.

       (i) Name **two** characteristics which affect the cost of a digital camera.

      (ii) Describe **two** advantages of using a digital camera compared to an ordinary photographic camera.   **3**

    (*c*) A printer has to be used so that the company can print out photographs. State **two** characteristics which this printer should have. Justify your answers.   **2**

    (*d*) The company wishes to create and distribute a searchable electronic catalogue of its best photographs. Describe how this could be done, mentioning any hardware or software required for the purpose.   **2**

Marks

SECTION II (continued)

16. A programmer has written a program which tests pupils on their knowledge of computer systems. A typical layout is shown below.

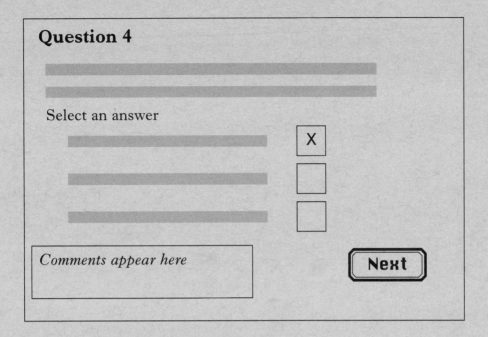

The program displays questions which have been stored in a disk file. The pupil selects an answer from a list of answers. The program then checks the answer entered by the pupil and displays a suitable comment. Data on the pupil's performance is saved to disk.

The difficulty of the questions can be altered by using a dialog box which appears when a menu option is selected from a pull down menu. Default settings are set up when the program loads.

(a) Describe **two** features of an event driven programming language which would make it particularly suitable for writing such a program.　　　2

(b) Another programmer suggests that a procedural language could be used to write this program.

How do procedural languages differ from event driven languages?　　　2

(c) The program uses calls to operating system functions while it is running.

Describe **two** functions of an operating system which the finished program described here would need to use.　　　2

(d) The program could also be created in some classes of applications package. Describe **two** advantages and **two** difficulties of using an applications package rather than a programming language to produce this program.

You do not have to describe in detail how to create the program in an applications package, but you may illustrate your answer with examples, referring to one or more class of package.　　　4

[Turn over

Marks

SECTION II (continued)

Attempt either Question 17 or Question 18

17. A program deals with the results of 10 tests taken by a computing student. The results are given as percentages.

   (a) State a *complex condition* which would be needed in an input validation procedure for the data.　　　　**1**

   (b) The program contains a number of procedures and functions.

   Describe **two** advantages of using parameter passing rather than global variables to allow data flow in the program.　　　　**2**

   (c) The programmer could use ten *variables* or a *one-dimensional array* to represent the results in the program.

   Compare these strategies in terms of:

   　(i)　use of storage space;

   　(ii)　readability of the program;

   　(iii)　parameter passing.　　　　**3**

   (d) When the program is written using a one-dimensional array, the data is passed to procedures as a parameter. Describe **two** differences between passing the list of results as a parameter *by reference* and *by value*.　　　　**4**

Marks

SECTION II (continued)

18. A program is being written that will search for a value in a list of integers. The program will report whether the value has been found together with the position of the first occurrence of the value in the list of integers. An appropriate error message will be reported if the value is not present in the list of integers.

    Below is a level 1 algorithm for this program.

    Steps of Level 1 Algorithm
    1 get search item
    2 search list of numbers for search item
    3 report findings

    (a) For step 2 in the algorithm above:

       (i) state the parameters required and their data types;

      (ii) for each parameter, state the parameter passing mechanism.   **3**

    (b) Step 2 needs to make use of a *complex condition* to control a conditional loop. Describe the complex condition needed in step 2.   **1**

    (c) The programmer has access to a module library which contains a suitable coded search algorithm to be used for step 2. Give **two** advantages, apart from saving time, of using the module library rather than coding it from scratch.   **2**

    (d) The programmer has decided to modify this algorithm to store the positions of **all** of the occurrences of the search item in the list of integers.

       (i) What change will be required in the loop in step 2?

      (ii) What additional data items will be required to store all of the positions where the search item is found?   **4**

[END OF SECTION II]

[Turn over

[BLANK PAGE]

SECTION III

Attempt ONE sub-section of Section III

Part A	Artificial Intelligence	Page 12	Questions 19 to 22
Part B	Computer Networking	Page 15	Questions 23 to 26
Part C	Computer Programming	Page 18	Questions 27 to 30
Part D	Multimedia Technology	Page 22	Questions 31 to 34

For the sub-section chosen, attempt three questions

the <u>first two</u> questions and <u>either</u> the third question <u>or</u> the fourth question.

[Turn over

SECTION III

Part A—Artificial Intelligence

Marks

**Attempt Question 19 and Question 20
and <u>either</u> Question 21 <u>or</u> Question 22**

19. A software company has been contracted to develop an expert system to advise sailors on weather forecasting.

   (*a*) (i) What stages in the development process should take place before implementation of the software?

   (ii) Describe clearly the roles of the knowledge engineer and domain experts in these stages.   **3**

   (*b*) (i) The company decides to use an expert system shell to implement the software. Clearly explain the difference between an *expert system* and an *expert system shell*.

   (ii) State **one** advantage and **one** disadvantage of using an expert system shell for the development compared with coding the expert system in a declarative language.   **3**

   (*c*) The following information is to be included in the expert system.

   > "Wind speed is very likely to increase if the wind direction is southerly and the air pressure is falling. Wind speed may increase if the wind direction is northerly and the air pressure is falling."

   (i) Design rules which could represent this information in a form with which you are familiar.

   (ii) Explain how your rules distinguish between "very likely" and "may".

   (iii) Describe **one** legal implication of this expert system being made available commercially.   **4**

Marks

SECTION III

Part A—Artificial Intelligence (continued)

20. The following knowledge base holds information about some British mountains.

```
1. mountain (snowdon,wales,3560)
2. mountain (scafell,england,3162)
3. mountain (ben_nevis,scotland,4406)
4. mountain (ben_lomond,scotland,3192)
5. mountain (hart_fell,scotland,2400)
6. munro (X)  if
   mountain (X,scotland,H)  and
   H>3000
```

Snowdon is a mountain in Wales which is 3560ft high etc

A Munro is a mountain in Scotland over 3000ft high

(*a*) (i) What would be the result of the following query?

```
?mountain (ben_nevis,X,Y)
```

   (ii) Write a query which would list all the mountains in Scotland.   2

(*b*) Assuming a depth-first search is used, explain how the program would find a solution to the following query.

```
?munro (ben_nevis)
```
                                                                             2

(*c*) A "furth" is a mountain over 3000ft high which is not in Scotland. Design a rule to represent this information.   2

(*d*) An alternative representation of the facts could be in the form:

```
height(snowdon,3560)
height(scafell,3162)
height(ben_nevis,4406)
height(ben_lomond,3192)
height(hart_fell,2400)

country(snowdon,wales)
country(scafell,england)
country(ben_nevis,scotland)
country(ben_lomond,scotland)
country(hart_fell,scotland)
```

   (i) Design a "munro" rule for use with this representation.

   (ii) The completed knowledge base will contain information about **all** British mountains. Explain a disadvantage of this second representation once the knowledge base is in operation.   4

[Turn over

Marks

SECTION III

Part A—Artificial Intelligence (continued)

Attempt either Question 21 or Question 22

21. Some of the earliest artificial intelligence research related to rule-based systems for playing strategic games such as chess which have a large number of game positions and possible moves.

    (a) Describe **two** difficulties in developing a rule-based system for playing chess.

    2

    (b) Name **two** hardware developments which allow modern chess playing systems to be much more successful than those of the 1960s and describe how the developments make this possible.

    2

    (c) Explain the purpose of *heuristics* in such rule-based systems.

    1

    (d) It could be argued that a rule-based system is not really intelligent. Describe a feature of a system which, if implemented, would justify the system being considered intelligent.

    2

    (e) A world chess champion has been beaten by a chess playing computer.

    (i) Describe another area of human ability where computer programs appear to show intelligence.

    (ii) "There are some areas of human ability where a computer program could never out-perform a human." Do you agree? Justify your answer.

    3

22. One area of successful artificial intelligence research is the development of artificial neural networks.

    (a) (i) State **one** limitation of an artificial neural network in comparison to a human brain.

    (ii) Describe how a neural network can be trained to display intelligent behaviour.

    (iii) Name an example of a successful use of neural networks in the "real world".

    (iv) State **one** objection to the use of neural networks in safety-critical applications.

    5

    (b) Another area of artificial intelligence research is the development of computer vision.

    (i) Describe **two** hardware developments that have contributed to the development of this area of artificial intelligence.

    (ii) Describe how computer vision can increase the effectiveness of industrial robots.

    (iii) Describe **one** other feature which would allow an industrial robot to be described as intelligent.

    5

[END OF SECTION III PART A]

SECTION III

Part B—Computer Networking

Marks

**Attempt Question 23 and Question 24
and <u>either</u> Question 25 <u>or</u> Question 26**

23. A newspaper journalist has a laptop computer and a digital camera. She can submit her stories and pictures from anywhere in the world by transferring data to the server in the central office.

   (*a*) List the hardware and software required to manage the communication between the laptop and the server computer and state the purpose of each item. **3**

   (*b*) (i) Explain the need for *communications protocols* in this situation.

       (ii) State **two** parameters which a protocol might define. **2**

   (*c*) (i) Explain the need for security in this situation.

       (ii) Describe **two** security measures which could be taken. **3**

   (*d*) In the central office, appropriate departments carry out further processing, such as text processing and digital image enhancement, on the journalist's files. These departments access the files from the server using the office local-area network (LAN).

   Describe **two** differences between the characteristics of the data communication on the office LAN compared to the journalist's original data transfer. **2**

24. A large company has a Glasgow office and an Edinburgh office which both have local-area networks (LANs) of desktop computers.

   The company want to connect the two LANs so that any computer on the Edinburgh LAN can access data which is stored on a server on the Glasgow LAN.

   The TCP/IP protocol stack will be used on all computers.

   (*a*) (i) State the hardware necessary to connect the two LANs.

       (ii) What is the name given to a network of this type? **2**

   (*b*) Describe how the TCP/IP protocols manage the transfer of a file between two computers on this network. **2**

   (*c*) The two LANs could be connected using a fixed leased line or ISDN. Describe **one** advantage and **one** disadvantage of **each** method. **2**

   (*d*) The company wants to provide information services by installing a Web server in one office. The information stored on the Web server will be accessed using Internet style software such as browsers.

       (i) Name a protocol which might be used to control the transfer of data from the Web server computer to the Web browser software and describe its purpose.

       (ii) Describe **one** advantage and **one** disadvantage of storing all of the information service data on a single server in one office rather than having two copies, one in each office. **4**

Marks

SECTION III

Part B—Computer Networking (continued)

Answer either Question 25 or Question 26

25. A school office has a local-area network of desktop computers. Each office worker has arranged for **one** folder on their local hard disk to be shared so that other workers can copy files out of that folder. This allows workers to transfer files and messages between their computers.

(a) (i) What name is given to this type of networking?

   (ii) How can each worker ensure that only certain workers can access the shared folder on their computer?

   (iii) How can they ensure that the other workers can only copy out of the folder and not into the folder?   **3**

(b) The school management have decided that it would be better to store all shared files on a central computer so that all office staff can access them from there. This was decided on the grounds of data security and data integrity.

   (i) What name is given to this type of networking?

   (ii) Name **one** additional item of software and **one** additional item of hardware that would be required to implement this new system.   **3**

(c) For the type of network described in part (b):

   (i) explain how this mode of networking provides data security and data integrity;

   (ii) describe an additional service which could be provided by this new networking mode and explain why it could not be provided before.   **4**

Marks

SECTION III

Part B—Computer Networking (continued)

26. A school pupil wants to obtain information on design notations used in software development as part of a homework exercise. She wants to use the Internet to find suitable information. To do this she must use communications software to connect to her Internet Service Provider.

    (a) Describe **two** functions of the communications software, other than dialling the telephone number of the Internet Service Provider.　　**2**

    (b) How can she locate a Web site containing descriptions of design notations used in software development if she does not know its URL?　　**2**

    (c) She finds a Web site which has the facility to download a document on the subject. When she clicks on the link, the following URL appears in the location bar of the browser software.

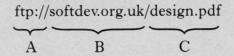

　　　ftp://softdev.org.uk/design.pdf
　　　　A　　　B　　　C

    Describe the purpose of the parts of URL labelled A, B and C.　　**2**

    (d) She finds that the file takes too long to download and decides to download it in school the next day as she knows that Web pages download faster at school.

    Give **two** reasons why Web pages might download faster at school.　　**2**

    (e) When she tries to download the file, she finds that ftp access has been barred.

    　　(i) Why might ftp access be barred by the school?

    　　(ii) What application on the school network has barred ftp access?　　**2**

[END OF SECTION III PART B]

[Turn over

SECTION III

Part C—Computer Programming

Marks

**Attempt Question 27 and Question 28
and either Question 29 or Question 30**

27. The positive integer 25 can be converted to binary by repeated division as follows.

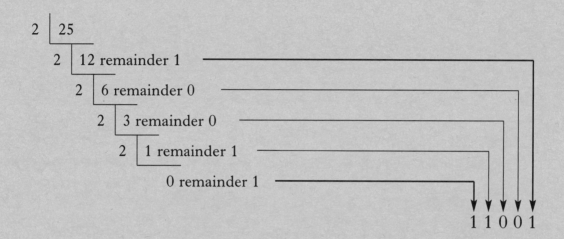

The binary value is obtained by arranging the remainders as shown.

In a program to teach pupils how this process works, the programmer wishes to store the 5 pairs of results (eg 12 and 1, 6 and 0 . . .) in a two-dimensional array.

(a) Describe fully how a *two-dimensional array* could be used to represent the results of each stage in converting a positive integer to binary.   2

(b) Describe in pseudocode, or otherwise, the process of assigning values to the two-dimensional array. State any limitations of your design.   4

(c) The same data could be represented using a one-dimensional array.

  (i) Describe how a one-dimensional array could represent this data.

  (ii) Explain how this would make the maintenance of the program more difficult.   4

SECTION III

Part C—Computer Programming (continued)

28. A program first reads a list of student names and corresponding examination marks from a text file held on disk. The student names and marks are stored and processed in the computer's memory using parallel one-dimensional arrays.

   (*a*) A run-time error could occur during the reading of the data from the file in this program.

   (i) State the type of run time error which could occur.

   (ii) Describe how the error could be detected and reported by the program so that the program does not crash.   **3**

   (*b*) Using pseudocode, or another suitable form, describe how data is read from the file and stored in the parallel arrays.   **3**

   (*c*) Student names are to be sorted into ascending alphabetic order.

   (i) What problem arises when sorting the parallel one-dimensional arrays?

   (ii) How would a record structure remove any problems?   **2**

   (*d*) An insert operation finds the correct position in the array at which to store a student name in alphabetic order.

   (i) State **two** conditions that the insert operation needs to test.

   (ii) Using a diagram, show how items are relocated when a new name is inserted.   **2**

[Turn over

Marks

SECTION III

Part C—Computer Programming (continued)

Answer either Question 29 or Question 30

29. Compilers have to be able to deal with arithmetic expressions such as

    (9 – 2) * (3 + 4)

    This kind of expression can be transformed into a sequence of symbols thus:

    9 2 – 3 4 + *

    This is then processed using a *stack data structure* with the following algorithm:

    ```
    loop
      get next symbol
      if symbol is a number then
        push symbol onto stack
      end if
      if symbol is an operator then
        pop the top two items from the stack and carry out the
          operation on these values
        push the result onto the stack
      end if
    end loop
    ```

    (a) Using a diagram, show the state of the stack after the symbol "3" has been *pushed* onto it. 2

    (b) Give the upper limit of the size of the stack needed in this case. 1

    (c) Describe, in pseudocode or otherwise, the operation to push a symbol onto the stack. You should mention the types of all data items needed. 3

    (d) A more complex arithmetic expression could cause an error if the size of the stack is set to the value you gave in (a) above.

     (i)   What is the name of this error condition?

     (ii) How could the program detect this condition?

     (iii) How could a program deal with this error if it occurs? 4

Marks

SECTION III

Part C—Computer Programming (continued)

30. A printer buffer uses a *queue data structure* to hold items of data that are to be printed. A queue data structure requires additional data items to support its operations.

(*a*) (i) What are the additional data items that are required?

(ii) When the printer buffer queue is full, what conditions will be true of the additional data items? **2**

(*b*) One of these conditions will cause a problem.

(i) State what the problem is.

(ii) Outline a solution to this problem. **3**

(*c*) Describe how an item is added to the printer buffer queue. You may use labelled diagrams to illustrate your answer. **2**

(*d*) Print *server* software stores a data record in a queue, rather than the data itself. The data record contains the username, timestamp and the name of the file in which the print job is stored.

This allows an administrator to manage the queue, by changing the order of items, removing items from the queue and getting status information.

Describe, in pseudocode or otherwise, a method of finding the number of items in a print server queue for a given user. **3**

[END OF SECTION III PART C]

[Turn over

SECTION III

Part D—Multimedia Technology

Marks

**Attempt Question 31 and Question 32
and <u>either</u> Question 33 <u>or</u> Question 34**

31. (*a*) (i) Explain what is meant by the term *authoring tool*.

      (ii) Describe **two** features of an authoring tool which enable the creation of a multimedia application.   **4**

(*b*) Recent developments in hardware and software technologies have contributed to the growth of multimedia. Explain how recent developments in
- optical data storage, and
- sound card technologies

have contributed to this growth.   **4**

(*c*) There are various standard file formats for digitised sound which allow the exchange of sounds between different software packages. Describe the features of **one** such audio file format.   **2**

32. Design of the layout is usually undertaken before constructing a multimedia presentation.

(*a*) State **three** elements of design layout which may be included in the planning of a multimedia presentation.   **3**

(*b*) Icon based and script based software are used to produce the presentation. Explain why a developer may wish to consider the use of a script based development tool within a multimedia authoring package.   **2**

(*c*) The quality of the final presentation may be limited by the display hardware.

      (i) State **three** characteristics of the display hardware which may affect the quality of the final presentation.

      (ii) Describe the role of the video graphics card in overcoming this problem above.   **5**

Marks

SECTION III

Part D—Multimedia Technology (continued)

Answer either Question 33 or Question 34

33. A company is producing a tourist information *presentation* comprising various media elements such as video, photographs, text and sound. One of the developers is working from home and communicating electronically with the company headquarters. The developer has scanned an image and saved the file in TIFF format.

    (*a*) (i) Two different types of scanner are being considered by the company which will allow the developer to scan text and graphics. Apart from cost, describe **two** characteristics which should be used when comparing **two** different types of scanner.

    (ii) Suggest a specification for a scanner for the purpose described. Justify your answer. 4

    (*b*) The scanning software by default saves scanned images in TIFF format. Name **one** other format and describe **one** advantage that TIFF has over your chosen format. 1

    (*c*) Once the digital images have been received by the company, image processing software is used to carry out further tasks. Describe **three** further image processing tasks that could be carried out. 3

    (*d*) Another developer is producing all the text based documents for the presentation. Compare **two** file formats in which the text documents could be sent electronically to the office for inclusion in the presentation. 2

34. (*a*) *File compression* is widely used with multimedia elements.

    (i) Name and describe **one** compression technique which can be used with multimedia data.

    (ii) Describe a multimedia situation where this technique may be applied. 3

    (*b*) Many graphics file formats are available to the multimedia designer for a variety of purposes. Name and describe the characteristics of **one** file format which comprises bit-mapped data and **one** file format which comprises vector data. 4

    (*c*) *Gamma correction* is one feature of graphic manipulation software which adjusts the gamma or mid tones of an image. Describe **three** other features used for manipulation of digitised images in software. 3

[END OF SECTION III PART D]

[END OF QUESTION PAPER]

[BLANK PAGE]

[BLANK PAGE]

Official SQA Past Papers: Higher Computing 2002

X017/301

NATIONAL
QUALIFICATIONS
2002

THURSDAY, 6 JUNE
1.00 PM – 3.30 PM

COMPUTING
HIGHER

Attempt **all** questions in Section I.

Attempt **four** questions in Section II

    Question 13 and Question 14
    and **either** Question 15 **or** Question 16
    and **either** Question 17 **or** Question 18

Attempt **one** sub-section of Section III.

Part A	Artificial Intelligence	Page 12	Questions 19 to 22
Part B	Computer Networking	Page 16	Questions 23 to 26
Part C	Computer Programming	Page 19	Questions 27 to 30
Part D	Multimedia Technology	Page 23	Questions 31 to 34

For the sub-section chosen, attempt **three** questions.

The **first two** questions and **either** the third question **or** the fourth question.

Read all questions carefully.

Do not write on the question paper.

Write as neatly as possible.

SCOTTISH
QUALIFICATIONS
AUTHORITY

MCB X017/301 6/8670

SECTION I

Attempt all questions in this section

Marks

1. (a) Give **two** reasons why computers use binary numbers to represent and store data. **2**

   (b) Which **one** of the following is the 8-bit two's complement representation of −14?

   (i) 11110001   (ii) 11110010   (iii) 10001110   (iv) 11110011   **1**

2. (a) Describe how *ASCII* is used to represent text. **1**

   (b) Explain what is meant by a *character set*. **1**

3. Modern computers use the *stored program concept*. Explain what is meant by the stored program concept and give **one** advantage of this aspect of computer design. **2**

4. State the purpose of:

   (i) *system software* and

   (ii) *application software*. **2**

5. (a) (i) State **two** hardware characteristics which could be used to compare a desktop computer and a network server.

   (ii) Use these characteristics to distinguish between a desktop computer and a network server. **3**

   (b) Describe **one** function which may be provided by a network operating system in addition to the standard functions of an operating system. **1**

6. State **two** functions of a peripheral device *interface* in a computer system. **2**

7. The software development process begins with the *analysis* stage and finishes with *maintenance*.

   (a) What is the purpose of the analysis stage? **1**

   (b) Name the document produced as a result of the analysis stage. **1**

   (c) There are **three** different types of maintenance which can be carried out on a piece of software once it is distributed. Name and describe each type. **3**

Marks

SECTION I (continued)

8. *Module libraries* are often used by programmers when they develop software.

    (*a*) What is a module library?   **1**

    (*b*) State **two** features which make modules *portable*.   **1**

    (*c*) Well-designed modules should be *robust* and *fit for purpose*.

    Explain each of these terms.   **2**

9. A school library has just bought a program to record book loans. One of the program's modules asks for the name of a book and returns the name of the pupil who has borrowed it. Which **one** of the following algorithms is most likely to be used in this module?

    •   Find minimum value
    •   Linear search
    •   Counting occurrences
    •   Input validation   **1**

10. Describe **two** features of a structured listing.   **2**

11. Parameter passing is one way of controlling the flow of data between procedures. Parameters may be *passed by value* or *passed by reference*.

    Explain what is meant by the term "passed by value" in relation to parameters.   **1**

12. The elimination of errors is a very important part of the software development process. *Syntax errors* and *logic errors* are two types of error which may occur.

    Use code from a programming environment with which you are familiar to illustrate **one** example of a syntax error and **one** example of a logic error.   **2**

    (30)

[END OF SECTION I]

[Turn over

SECTION II

Attempt FOUR questions in this section *Marks*

Question 13 and Question 14
and <u>either</u> Question 15 <u>or</u> Question 16
and <u>either</u> Question 17 <u>or</u> Question 18

13. The following diagram shows the basic design of a central processing unit. It has a 24-bit address bus and a 16-bit data bus.

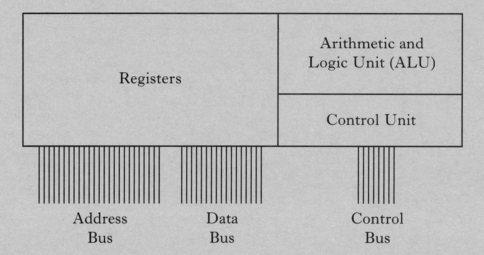

(*a*) A processor can be considered to be made up of **three** components: the *Arithmetic and Logic Unit* (*ALU*), the *Control Unit* and *registers*.

Describe the purpose of each of these components. **3**

(*b*) If a processor needs an instruction from memory, a read operation is carried out. Describe the steps of the *memory read* operation with reference to the processor, memory and buses. **3**

(*c*) *Throughput* is one way of measuring a computer's processing power.

Describe **two** developments in the internal organisation of computers which have increased throughput. **2**

(*d*) Calculate the maximum amount of addressable memory which the above processor could access.

Express your answer in appropriate units. **2**

Marks

SECTION II (continued)

14. Software has to be developed for a business which will allow the automatic processing of wages. A programmer has designed a structure chart as part of the design stage of the software development process.

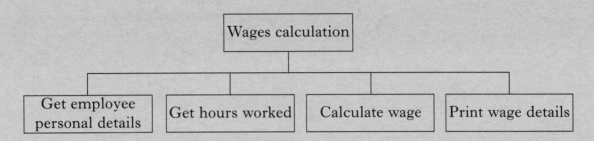

(a) Describe **one other** design technique which the programmer could use.   1

(b) Describe **one** software development tool the programmer could use during the development of this program **and** state the stage in the software development process at which it could be used.   2

(c) Describe **two** factors which will contribute to the choice of programming language used to implement the program.   2

(d) Describe **two** methods the programmer could use in order to make the program readable.   2

(e) For the "Get hours worked" procedure, give **three** items of test data the programmer could use to test this procedure fully.

Give **one** reason for **each** of your choices.   3

[Turn over

Marks

SECTION II (continued)

Attempt either Question 15 or Question 16

15. Kingsland Drive Youth Club has decided to set up a computer system so that they can send regular newsletters to members, and keep an up-to-date list of members' details and subscriptions.

    (a) List **three** types of application software they may need and describe the purpose of each type in this situation.   2

    (b) Articles for the newsletter will be provided in electronic form by members. Explain the importance of *data standards* in this situation.   2

    (c) *Input validation* is a feature provided by some application packages.

    Describe how the club could use application software to validate members' details as they are entered.   1

    (d) The newsletter will contain pictures of members of the club. There is not enough money to buy both a digital camera and a scanner.

    Which one would you recommend? Justify your answer, giving **two** advantages of your recommendation.   2

    (e) The club decides to buy a software package which includes a *scripting language*.

    (i) What is meant by the term "scripting language"?

    (ii) Describe a situation where the use of a scripting language would be helpful to the youth club.   3

Marks

SECTION II (continued)

16. A home computer system is advertised as having a standard operating system, a selection of utility programs and some additional bundled software.

(a) Describe **three** functions of a standard operating system. 2

(b) Describe **two** types of utility program which might be included. 2

(c) In addition to an internal 20 Gb hard disc drive, a 1·4 Mb floppy disc drive and a 48-speed CD-ROM drive, the buyer can specify one additional storage device.

   (i) Name **one** other storage device which could be useful to a home user.

   (ii) Describe a situation in which this device would be necessary.

      Justify your answer. 2

(d) Among the bundled software, the user finds an "intelligent chess tutor". Name a programming language suitable for developing programs which show "intelligence" and describe how this language differs from a procedural language. 2

(e) Explain **why** a program developer may use both an interpreter and a compiler in the development of a piece of software. 2

[Turn over

Marks

SECTION II (continued)

Attempt either Question 17 or Question 18

17. A program has been written to process a list of grades obtained by all pupils in Scotland who sat an examination. Grades are integers from 1 to 7 where 1 is the highest grade and 7 is the lowest. One of the program's functions is to count the number of pupils who obtained a grade 3, 4, 5 or 6.

A procedure is being written to carry out this function.

Here is a description of the procedure.

procedure to count number of pupils obtaining grades in a specified range

input parameters:	**upper_grade, lower_grade, list_of_grades**
output parameter:	**number_of_pupils**
process:	**the procedure will count the number of grades which are between upper_grade and lower_grade inclusive.**

(a) Describe **two** advantages of using *modularity* within programs.

2

(b) Why does the procedure use the parameters "upper_grade" and "lower_grade" rather than using the numbers "3" and "6"?

1

(c) (i) The parameters "upper_grade" and "lower_grade" could be defined as type integer or real.

Give **two** reasons why it would be better to define them as integer rather than real.

(ii) What data structure could be used to store the list of grades?

3

(d) Describe a *complex condition* which this procedure will need to use to identify the grades which are to be counted.

2

(e) The number of grades in the list is not known in advance.

Describe how a programmer can ensure that all grades are read and processed. You may illustrate your answer with pseudocode, or another design notation, or actual code from a programming language with which you are familiar.

2

Marks

SECTION II (continued)

18. A program is being written to analyse the number of road traffic accidents in six areas of Scotland. The names of the areas and the number of accidents are stored in two separate arrays. One of the program's functions is to find the area with the highest number of accidents.

Here is a possible algorithm for this part of the program.

find area with highest number of accidents

1 find position of maximum number in accidents array

2 print name from corresponding position in area array

(a) The design of the *user interface* is an important part of software design.

Describe **two** characteristics of a good user interface. 2

(b) Step 1 requires **two** parameters. Identify these parameters and state their data types and methods of parameter passing. 2

(c) Give **one** example of a possible use of a local variable in step 1 and explain why it should be a local variable rather than a global variable. 2

(d) Step 1 will require an *iteration* control structure and a *selection* control structure.

   (i) Describe **two** control structures which could be used.

   (ii) Show how these structures would be used to find the position of the maximum number in the accidents array. You may use pseudocode or another design notation or code from a programming language with which you are familiar. 4

[END OF SECTION II]

[Turn over

[BLANK PAGE]

SECTION III

Attempt ONE sub-section of Section III

Part A	Artificial Intelligence	Page 12	Questions 19 to 22
Part B	Computer Networking	Page 16	Questions 23 to 26
Part C	Computer Programming	Page 19	Questions 27 to 30
Part D	Multimedia Technology	Page 23	Questions 31 to 34

For the sub-section chosen, attempt three questions

the <u>first two</u> questions and <u>either</u> the third question <u>or</u> the fourth question.

[Turn over

SECTION III

Part A—Artificial Intelligence

Marks

Attempt Question 19 and Question 20
and <u>either</u> Question 21 <u>or</u> Question 22

19. Tony Wilson is a Countryside Ranger involved with the protection of endangered species in Scotland. He has asked Dr Natalie Ridge, a computer specialist, to help him create an expert system, called BatSearch, to help local volunteer groups learn how to identify seven species of bat in Scotland.

    (*a*) The first phase in the creation of the expert system involves Tony telling Dr Ridge how to identify Scottish bats.

       (i) Tony is the domain expert. Identify the role Dr Ridge is playing.

       (ii) Why are both Tony and Dr Ridge required at the *analysis* stage? **3**

    (*b*) An expert system consists of three distinct components.

    The *user interface* is one of them.

    Name and describe the purpose of the **other two** components. **3**

    (*c*) Dr Ridge asks if Tony would like to include *justification of reasoning*. Tony agrees that this would be useful. He also tells her to add a warning that it is against the law to handle live bats or to enter a roost unless you have a licence to do so.

       (i) What is meant by "justification of reasoning"?

       (ii) Why is this justification useful to the user of BatSearch?

       (iii) Explain why the information about handling live bats must be included as part of the system. **3**

    (*d*) At what later stage in the development process is Tony involved?

    Give a reason for your answer. **1**

Marks

SECTION III

Part A—Artificial Intelligence (continued)

20. Natural language processing is a fast growing area in artificial intelligence. Below is part of a program which is used to analyse sentence structure in order to work out what the sentence means. The program is written in a *declarative language* which uses *depth first search*.

```
 1   noun (badger)          badger is a noun
 2   noun (fox)
 3   noun (otter)

 4   verb (sees)            sees is a verb
 5   verb (jumps)
 6   verb (meets)

 7   adjective (brown)      brown is an adjective
 8   adjective (quick)
 9   adjective (lazy)

10   sentence (A B C) if
     noun (A) and          A sentence is a noun
     verb (B) and          followed by a verb
     noun (C)              followed by a noun
```

(a) (i) What would be the output from the following query?

?sentence (badger meets otter)

(ii) Explain how the system would evaluate the query.　　3

(b) The first solution for the query ?sentence (A sees C) is

A = badger, C = badger.

(i) What is the **second** solution?

(ii) Describe how you would alter the sentence rule so that the nouns are always different and sentences like **"badger sees badger"** are no longer valid.　　3

(c) Using the syntax above, write a rule called "complex_sentence" which would allow a sentence such as:

"lazy badger meets brown fox".　　2

(d) What difficulties would be encountered if the system were to be expanded to analyse all possible English sentences?　　2

[Turn over

Marks

SECTION III

Part A—Artificial Intelligence (continued)

Attempt <u>either</u> Question 21 <u>or</u> Question 22

21. Artificial Intelligence (AI) programs are often used in problem solving situations where the number of possible outcomes is large. One such area is in the design of processors. For example, a program might search through every possible design, examining each in turn to see which is the most efficient.

    (a) Two common search methods are *depth-first* and *breadth-first*. Describe how these search methods differ in their execution.

    You may use a diagram to illustrate your answer.   **3**

    (b) A well-chosen *heuristic* might be used to make the search more efficient.

    (i) Explain the term "heuristic".

    (ii) How would a well-chosen heuristic aid efficiency?   **2**

    AI might also have a role to play in the automated manufacture of circuit boards, through the use of visual recognition systems.

    (c) (i) Describe how the introduction of such a system might aid the manufacturing process.   **3**

    (ii) Give **one** financial advantage of introducing such a system.

    (d) The recognition system could be implemented in one of two ways:

    • using a *procedural language* like C
    • using a *declarative language* like Prolog or Lisp.

    Choose **one** of these development environments and give **one** advantage and **one** disadvantage of your choice compared to the alternative environment.   **2**

Marks

SECTION III

Part A—Artificial Intelligence (continued)

22. Recent advances in the use of *certainty factors* have allowed developers to mimic the thought processes of humans more closely.

    (a) Explain what is meant by "certainty factors". **1**

    (b) (i) Give a brief description of a medical or industrial application where certainty factors may be used to improve expert systems.

    (ii) Describe a possible legal implication which might arise from the use of this type of application. **3**

    (c) Describe the effects upon the field of Artificial Intelligence (AI) of **two** technological advances in hardware over the past two decades. Your answer should clearly show how these advances have aided the development of AI. **2**

    (d) One area of research is *computer vision*. Describe **two** aspects of human vision which are difficult to replicate in a computer vision system. **2**

    (e) Explain in detail how a neural network that is used in recognising postcodes can improve in performance over time. **2**

[END OF SECTION III PART A]

SECTION III

Part B—Computer Networking

Marks

**Attempt Question 23 and Question 24
and <u>either</u> Question 25 <u>or</u> Question 26**

23. Ettrickbank College is planning the installation of 200 new computer workstations. Unlike its original suite of computers, these will be networked.

   (a) Describe **one** economic factor and **one** technical factor which have led to the development of computer networking.   2

   (b) In addition to the 200 workstations, three servers will be required. One of these will be a *fileserver*.

       (i) Name **two** other types of server which are likely to be needed.

       (ii) Describe the function of each type.   2

   (c) State whether the network described above is a *peer-to-peer* or a *client-server* network. Justify your answer.   1

   (d) Explain **how** the security of user files may be ensured in this network.   2

   (e)   (i) Explain **why** a backup strategy is necessary for this network.

       (ii) Describe a suitable backup strategy, and explain how it could be implemented.   3

24. (a) Describe the purpose of each of the following devices in networking:

       (i) a *repeater*

       (ii) a *bridge*

       (iii) a *router*.   3

   (b) International *protocols,* such as FTP and SMTP, are vital for successful networking.

       (i) Describe the purpose of each of these protocols.

       (ii) Explain why international protocols are required.   3

   (c) A self-employed plumber has created a simple Web site advertising his services. He wants his site to "go live" on the Internet. Two possible URLs for the site are:

   www.billtheplumber.co.uk, or

   www.freewebservice.com/users/pages/billtheplumber.

   Describe **one** advantage and **one** disadvantage of each URL.   2

   (d) Describe how facilities provided by the Internet could:

       (i) benefit a small business such as a self-employed plumber

       (ii) cause difficulties for a small business.   2

Marks

SECTION III

Part B—Computer Networking (continued)

Answer either Question 25 or Question 26

25.   Five computers have been donated to Millside Library for public use.

   (*a*)   Describe **two** advantages of networking these computers within the library.   **2**

   (*b*)   State **one** additional item of hardware and **one** additional item of software which will need to be installed in the stand-alone computers if they are to be networked.   Describe the purpose of each item.   **2**

   (*c*)   A star topology has been chosen for the network.

     (i)   State **one** advantage of a star topology compared with a bus topology.

     (ii)   What **additional** item of hardware will be required to implement a star network? Explain why this will be necessary.

     (iii)   Name **two** types of cabling which may be used in networking.

       Which one would you recommend to connect the computers within the library? Give a reason for your choice.   **4**

   (*d*)   It is proposed to connect Millside Library's network to Millside High School's network.

     (i)   Why is this described as an *internetwork* rather than a wide area network?

     (ii)   Describe **one** benefit this could bring to the library users and **one** benefit it could bring to the school pupils.   **2**

[Turn over

Marks

SECTION III

Part B—Computer Networking (continued)

26. ScotWest Bank plc has 20 branches located throughout Scotland and a head office in Glasgow. Each branch has a local area network (LAN), and the branches and head office are connected by a wide area network (WAN).

    (*a*) Distinguish between a LAN and a WAN in terms of

       (i) bandwidth

       (ii) transmission media. 2

    (*b*) Describe **two** ways of ensuring security when financial data is being transferred between a branch and head office. 2

    (*c*) Explain how the increased use of computer networks in the banking industry has brought benefits to:

       (i) customers

       (ii) staff. 2

    (*d*) As a result of increased use of networking, the bank has long-term plans to close many of its branches. Customers complain that they will miss the opportunity to talk "face to face" with bank staff.

       (i) Describe a technological solution to this difficulty.

       (ii) Describe the specific hardware and software each customer would require (in **addition** to a computer) to implement your solution. 4

[END OF SECTION III PART B]

SECTION III

Part C—Computer Programming

Marks

**Attempt Question 27 and Question 28
and <u>either</u> Question 29 <u>or</u> Question 30**

27. The following names have been stored in an array as part of a personal organiser program which is being developed by a team of programmers.

> John
> Mary
> Alan
> Peter
> Gordon

The programmers want to add a search feature to the program so that a person's name can be found quickly.

It has been decided that a *binary search* will be used.

(*a*) (i) What would need to be done to the list of names once a *binary search* has been chosen?

    (ii) Why is this necessary?   **2**

(*b*) State **three** data items which would be required in addition to the list of names to implement the *binary search algorithm* and explain how these data items are used in the algorithm.   **3**

(*c*) Use the list of numbers

12, 15, 19, 23, 29

to compare the performance of the *binary search algorithm* with the *linear search algorithm* when the number 23 is to be found.   **2**

(*d*) In what circumstances would the *linear search algorithm* out-perform the *binary search algorithm*? Explain your answer.   **2**

(*e*) Explain why the efficiency of the search algorithm is important if the program is to be used on a palmtop computer.   **1**

[Turn over

Marks

SECTION III

Part C—Computer Programming (continued)

28. Fruitbat Software have been asked to implement a new set of card games. The cards are each to be represented by a code as shown below:

Ace of Clubs is AC

Ten of Diamonds is 10 D

King of Spades is KS

Five of Hearts is 5H

(a) One of the games involves dealing 13 cards into a separate pile to be used during the game. This pile is called the "bank".

The programmer has decided to use an *array* to represent the bank.

(i) What **size** and **type** of array should be used for the bank?

(ii) State **two** advantages of holding the bank using an array rather than as a series of variables.　　　　3

(b) Two complex data structures available to the programmer are a *stack* and a *queue*. Explain the difference between these two structures.　　　　2

(c) The array operates as a *stack*. As the game is played, cards are removed from the bank. When a card is removed from the bank, its code is *popped* from the top of the *stack*.

Card is popped

Describe, in pseudocode or otherwise, the process of popping a card from the stack.　　　　3

(d) One of the required features of the new software is the ability to save the bank to file. Describe, in pseudocode or otherwise, the process of saving the bank into a file.　　　　2

Marks

SECTION III

Part C—Computer Programming (continued)

Answer either Question 29 or Question 30

29. At a canoe slalom event, competitors are timed on a section of river. They set off at two minute intervals. At the finishing line, a judge writes down each competitor's name, bib number, time and penalty points. After three competitors have completed the course, the judge's notes look like this:

Name	*Bib number*	*Time (seconds)*	*Penalty points*
J Ashcroft	273	127·4	15
N Khan	185	153·2	10
S Buchanan	99	187·4	45

The judge is to be provided with a laptop computer running a specially designed program. This will allow each competitor's name, bib number, time and penalties to be entered as they finish, and stored in a file on disc.

(a) Name **two** file operations which will be required by the program, and explain why they are needed.　　2

(b) Each competitor's results are stored as a *record* in the file. Describe, in detail, a suitable record structure for this data.　　2

(c) Once all the results have been stored, they must be sorted into ascending order of the competitor's time.

　(i) Name **one** sort algorithm which could be used.

　(ii) Describe how this sort algorithm works. You may use a diagram, pseudocode or any other suitable form.　　3

(d) Name **one other** sort algorithm, and compare it with the one chosen in (c) in terms of:

　(i) use of memory

　(ii) use of processor time.　　2

(e) Explain why the three sets of results given in the table above would be inadequate test data to test this program.　　1

[Turn over

Marks

SECTION III

Part C—Computer Programming (continued)

30. The weather station at Loch Dubh has recorded the level of monthly rainfall in the area for 20 years from 1980 to 1999.

Here is a sample of the data for the years 1990 and 1991.

Year	Rainfall (in cm)											
	Jan	Feb	Mar	Apr	May	Jun	Jul	Aug	Sept	Oct	Nov	Dec
.	.	.	.	.	.	.	.	.	.	.	.	.
.	.	.	.	.	.	.	.	.	.	.	.	.
1990	10·3	9·3	9·8	15·1	13·4	4·1	2·3	4·3	6·7	6·8	9·8	7·6
1991	11·3	21·1	5·8	12·7	16·3	7·4	3·2	4·6	7·1	7·2	8·6	10·3
.	.	.	.	.	.	.	.	.	.	.	.	.
.	.	.	.	.	.	.	.	.	.	.	.	.

(a) Define a two dimensional array to store **all** of the data.   1

(b) The staff at the weather station want to know how many times the rainfall was greater than 10 cm.

   (i) Describe, using pseudocode or otherwise, how the number of months when the rainfall was over 10 cm could be calculated for a single year.

   (ii) Describe the changes which would need to be made to the algorithm to perform this calculation for the 20 year period.   4

(c) The maximum monthly rainfall for each year has to be found.

Describe how this could be done for each year using a one-dimensional array to store the results.   3

(d) The weather station wants to record the monthly rainfall for the next 20 years and continue making comparisons between months.

Describe **two** specific examples of *perfective maintenance* which would need to be made to the program.   2

[END OF SECTION III PART C]

SECTION III

Part D—Multimedia Technology

Marks

**Attempt Question 31 and Question 32
and <u>either</u> Question 33 <u>or</u> Question 34**

31. Over the last 20 years there has been a huge increase in the development of multimedia related hardware and software. *Hypermedia* and *Computer Based Training* are both applications of multimedia technology.

   (*a*) Hypermedia systems have developed from *hypertext* systems.

      (i) Describe **one** feature common to both systems.

      (ii) Describe **one** extra feature you would expect to find in a hypermedia system.

         2

   (*b*) Many businesses are now using Computer Based Training instead of traditional training methods.

      (i) Describe a situation where Computer Based Training would be useful.

      (ii) Describe **one** advantage of using Computer Based Training rather than traditional training methods in this situation.

         2

   (*c*) A hardware specification is being developed for a Computer Based Training system.

      (i) Describe **two** advantages of using a DVD instead of a CD-ROM in this situation.

      (ii) Describe **two** characteristics of display hardware and explain how they will affect the quality of the Computer Based Training presentation.

      (iii) The development team has been told that the budget will allow either a faster processor or additional RAM to be purchased. Which upgrade would you recommend? Justify your answer.

         6

[Turn over

SECTION III

Part D—Multimedia Technology (continued)

Marks

32. A multimedia designer has been employed to create a multimedia project for a local bus company. The designer has created a design of the home page below.

```
┌─────────────────────────────────────────────────────┐
│  ┌─────────────┐   ┌───────────────────────────────┐ │
│  │ Video of    │   │                               │ │
│  │ company     │   │      Company's logo           │ │
│  │ buses in    │   └───────────────────────────────┘ │
│  │ action      │   ┌───────────────────────────────┐ │
│  │             │   │ Description of bus routes     │ │
│  │             │   │ and bus timetables with       │ │
│  │             │   │ hyperlinks to other pages for │ │
│  │             │   │ further information           │ │
│  │             │   │                               │ │
│  │             │   │                               │ │
│  └─────────────┘   └───────────────────────────────┘ │
└─────────────────────────────────────────────────────┘
```

(a) The designer begins by making a *storyboard* of the whole multimedia presentation.

What is a storyboard and how will it help the implementation of the presentation?　2

(b) The designer is aware that the multimedia pages could be developed using either an *icon-based* or a *script-based* package.

Which one would you recommend to the designer? Explain your choice.　2

(c) In addition to a computer system, name **two** items of hardware the designer may have to use to produce this home page and **describe the function** of **each** item.　2

(d) The designer has decided that the home page should include a feature which enables the user to hear the bus times and routes.

Explain how this could be done. Your explanation should include a description of any software and hardware which will be required.　3

(e) Explain the importance of MPC standards when designing multimedia presentations.　1

Marks

SECTION III

Part D—Multimedia Technology (continued)

Answer either Question 33 or Question 34

33. A small photography business has created a presentation of its best photographs. These photographs can be viewed on the computers in the company's shops.

    (a) Name **two** possible hardware devices which could capture the photographs. Describe how each device would be used. **2**

    (b) There are different techniques which may be used to store photographs.

        (i) Explain the difference between *lossy* and *lossless* compression.

        (ii) Name **two** standard file formats which could be used to store the photographs. Which one would you recommend? Justify your answer. **3**

    (c) One of the services provided by the company is the ability to "enhance" customers' photographs.

        Describe **three** features of graphic manipulation software which the company might use to provide this service. **3**

    (d) The company now wishes to create a magazine of its best photographs to send to customers. Instead of using a word processing package they decide to use a desk top publishing package.

        Describe **two** advantages of using a desk top publishing package rather than a word processing package to produce the magazine. **2**

34. Using synthesised music is an important part of the popular music industry today.

    (a) Describe how the Musical Instrument Digital Interface (MIDI) has contributed to this development. **2**

    (b) Describe the difference between *Frequency Modulation* and *Wave Table Synthesis*. **2**

    (c) *Compression* and *sampling rates* are important factors in audio processing.

        (i) Describe what is meant by the terms "compression" and "sampling rate".

        (ii) Name and describe **two** different audio file formats.

        (iii) Explain why it is necessary to use a sampling rate which is neither too low nor too high when recording sound. **6**

[END OF SECTION III PART D]

[END OF QUESTION PAPER]

[BLANK PAGE]

[BLANK PAGE]

X017/301

NATIONAL QUALIFICATIONS 2003	THURSDAY, 22 MAY 1.00 PM – 3.30 PM	COMPUTING HIGHER

Attempt **all** questions in Section I.

Attempt **four** questions in Section II

    Question 14 and Question 15
    and **either** Question 16 **or** Question 17
    and **either** Question 18 **or** Question 19

Attempt **one** sub-section of Section III.

Part A	Artificial Intelligence	Page 12	Questions 20 to 23
Part B	Computer Networking	Page 15	Questions 24 to 27
Part C	Computer Programming	Page 17	Questions 28 to 31
Part D	Multimedia Technology	Page 21	Questions 32 to 35

For the sub-section chosen, attempt **three** questions.

The **first two** questions and **either** the third question **or** the fourth question.

Read all questions carefully.

Do not write on the question paper.

Write as neatly as possible.

SCOTTISH
QUALIFICATIONS
AUTHORITY

SECTION I

Attempt all questions in this section

Marks

1. Describe **three** different types of software maintenance.

    3

2. During the implementation stage in any software development project, the target is to deliver code which is <u>correct</u> and <u>reliable</u>.

    Explain **both** of the underlined terms.

    2

3. When producing software, it is very important to have good design and clear documentation.

    (*a*) (i) Name **two** methods of representing program design.

         (ii) Give **one** advantage of **each** method.

    3

    (*b*) Describe **two** items of documentation that would accompany the finished software.

    2

4. *Fixed loops* and *conditional loops* are types of *iterative* control structures.

    (*a*) Describe a conditional loop. You may use an example from a programming language with which you are familiar.

    1

    (*b*) What is the difference between a fixed loop and a conditional loop?

    1

    (*c*) Explain the meaning of "iterative" in relation to control structures.

    1

5. A *readable* program is easier to maintain.

    (*a*) Explain why a readable program is easier to maintain.

    1

    (*b*) State **two** techniques that programmers could use to make their programs more readable.

    1

6. (*a*) What feature of computer architecture determines *word size*?

    1

    (*b*) Explain how word size affects system performance.

    1

7. The processor and memory are linked by the *address*, *data* and *control buses*.

    Give **two** examples of the use of the control bus.

    1

8. A company logo has been created in both *vector* and *bit-mapped* graphics packages. Describe **two** actions which could be carried out on the "vector graphic" but not on the "bit-mapped graphic".

    2

9. *Signed-bit* and *two's complement* are two ways of storing binary integers. Give **two** advantages of using two's complement rather than signed-bit.

    2

Marks

SECTION I (continued)

10. (*a*) (i) State **one** network topology that could be used for a local area network.

      (ii) Draw a labelled diagram of this topology.   1

    (*b*) What would be the result of channel failure in your chosen topology?   1

11. State **one** similarity and **one** difference between *scripting* and *procedural* programming languages.   2

12. *Resolution* and *capacity* are important features of digital cameras.

    (*a*) Explain the terms "resolution" and "capacity" in relation to digital cameras.   1

    (*b*) Describe how the resolution of a digital camera affects its capacity.   1

13. Standard file formats are often used to transfer data between applications packages of the same type.

    Choose **two** different types of application package and state **one** standard file format for each.   2

                                                                   (30)

[END OF SECTION I]

[Turn over

SECTION II

Attempt FOUR questions in this section

Marks

Question 14 and Question 15
and either Question 16 or Question 17
and either Question 18 or Question 19

14. Most computers are still based on the system proposed by John von Neumann.

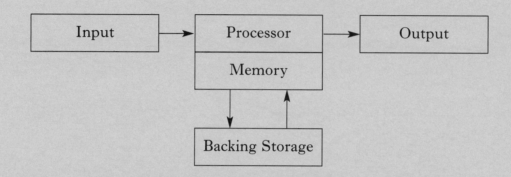

(a) (i) Explain how memory is organised so that data can be stored and retrieved by the processor.

(ii) Explain the importance of the *memory management* function of the operating system.

2

(b) *Registers* are one component of the processor.

(i) Explain how the number of registers can affect system performance.

(ii) Name **one** other component of the processor and describe its function.

2

(c) Different types of memory can be used within a computer system such as *ROM*, *RAM*, *SRAM* and *DRAM*.

(i) Explain why *maintainability* of ROM-based software could pose problems.

(ii) Describe **one** solution to this problem not involving the use of RAM.

(iii) Describe **one** advantage and **one** disadvantage of using DRAM instead of SRAM other than cost.

4

(d) A computer system with a microprocessor which has a 24-bit data bus and a 32-bit address bus is sold with 1Gb of addressable memory. What is the maximum amount of **additional** memory which could be added to this computer system?

Express your answer using appropriate units.

2

Marks

SECTION II (continued)

15. A software company has been asked to create a piece of software to help an employment agency match various jobs with prospective employees. The software company carries out an analysis on how the agency currently performs this task.

    (a) Describe **one** method that the software company might have used to analyse the agency's current system. 1

    The software will store the responses of applicants to a number of standard questions. The applicants' responses are whole numbers in the range 1 to 5.

    (b) The set of responses given by the applicants must be held during processing. These are held in an *array of integers*. Give **two** reasons why an array has been chosen to hold the responses. 2

    (c) When the array is searched, the module responsible returns the location of where the item is found. The search item can be passed as a parameter either *by reference* or *by value*.

        (i) Explain the terms "pass by reference" and "pass by value".

        (ii) Which is more appropriate for passing the search item? Justify your choice. 3

    (d) The software development team could have chosen to implement the program in a **declarative** language.

        Explain why they might have considered this approach. 2

    (e) Good documentation should be developed both at the *implementation* stage and at the *testing* stage of the software development process.

        Describe how documentation from **each** of these stages can benefit *maintainability*. 2

[Turn over

Marks

SECTION II (continued)

Attempt either Question 16 or Question 17

16. A publishing business uses a range of computer systems, software and peripherals to produce its newspapers and magazines.

    (*a*) Name a type of software application it could choose for creating a newspaper and give **one** reason for your choice.

    1

    (*b*) A high resolution scanner is used to capture photographs onto a computer.

      (i) Describe **two** hardware features of a scanner, other than resolution.

      (ii) Calculate how much storage would be required for a 6 ↔ 4 inch photograph scanned at 600 dpi using 256 colours.

      Express your answer in appropriate units.

    4

    (*c*) (i) The business wants to equip its journalists with either laptop or palmtop computers. Which computer system would you recommend? Give **one hardware** and **one software** reason for your choice.

      (ii) Describe how the *user interface* of your recommended system could benefit the journalist.

    3

    (*d*) The business decides to invest in a piece of software which will allow readers to search for past news stories using keywords. Give **one** advantage and **one** disadvantage to the software house of using a general-purpose database package to create this software rather than creating a specialised software package.

    2

SECTION II (continued)

17. Panes 2001 is a stand-alone operating system. It boasts many features such as:

    • Plug and play

    • Graphical user interface

    • Utility software

    • Multimedia features.

    (*a*) Why does a computer require an operating system?　　　　　　　　　　**1**

    (*b*) What is *utility software*? Describe **one** utility which may be provided with Panes 2001.　　　　　　　　　　**2**

    (*c*) In order to use multimedia elements (such as text, graphics, video and sound), *standard file formats* have to be used by the software.

    　　　Why are standard file formats necessary?　　　　　　　　　　**1**

    (*d*) One of the system requirements for Panes 2001 is that it requires 256 Mb of RAM. Describe **two** other **hardware** requirements which may be necessary for a computer to run an operating system such as Panes 2001.　　　　　　　　　　**2**

    (*e*) An upgrade to Panes 2001 is to include many extra features including video manipulation and voice recognition.

    　　(i) Explain how the use of modular programming in Panes 2001 could benefit the coding of these new features.

    　　(ii) Describe **two** methods that programmers could use at the testing stage to ensure that the upgrade is free from errors.　　　　　　　　　　**4**

[Turn over

Marks

SECTION II (continued)

Attempt either Question 18 or Question 19

18. The Scottish Tree Foundation has commissioned a piece of software to be written to gather information for a national survey of trees in Scotland. The prototypes of two styles of user interface are shown below.

Interface A

```
Please enter tree name . . .
?|
```

Interface B

```
Please choose the tree name        OK
from the list and press OK

  Oak, Black        ▲
  Oak, Holm
  Oak, Sessile
  Pear, Common      ☐
  Pear, Willow-leaved  ▼
```

Using this program, data is gathered and output to a text file for processing later.

(a) Describe **each** of the interfaces in terms of *robustness*, *ease of data entry* and *efficiency of computer resources*. 3

(b) Describe **two** features of an *event driven* language which would make it easier to implement Interface B compared with using a procedural language. 2

(c) The software must be run on a number of different computer systems. Describe **two** ways in which the software company could make the program *portable*. 2

(d) It is suggested that the time required to develop the program might be reduced by the use of a module library.

How might the use of a *module library* accelerate the development process? 1

(e) One module of the program will take a tree name from the user and will count all occurrences of that name in the current list of trees. The module will return the number of times the name appears in the list or zero if the name is not found. Using pseudocode or otherwise, write a detailed algorithm for this process. 2

Marks

SECTION II (continued)

19. A large suite of software consisting of separate modules is being developed by several programming teams. A number of stages are gone through to ensure that these modules will fit together properly.

(a) Individual programmers can take steps during the writing of these modules that will make the modules fit together more easily. A program can be made more *robust* by using local variables instead of global variables where possible.

   (i) Explain the difference between *global variables* and *local variables*.

   (ii) How would the use of local variables contribute to the "robustness" of the software? **3**

(b) The type of programming language used for software implementation must be decided at an early stage in the design process.

   Describe **three** factors, other than the expertise of the programmers, which will affect the final choice of language for the implementation. **3**

The software is able to have several windows open at once. The program holds a list of the names of all open windows in an appropriate data structure.

(c) What type of data structure is being used to hold the names? Your answer should state the **full** data type of the data structure. **1**

When a window is selected, a software module finds the position of that window in the list. For example, when the user clicks on a window, the module checks the list and returns its position in the list.

(d) Use pseudocode, or another design notation of your choice, to fully describe the process of identifying the position of the name in the list. **2**

(e) When the software is handling the window selection process described above, it communicates with part of the operating system. Which part of the operating system is involved? Justify your answer. **1**

[*END OF SECTION II*]

[Turn over

[BLANK PAGE]

SECTION III

Attempt ONE sub-section of Section III

Part A	Artificial Intelligence	Page 12	Questions 20 to 23
Part B	Computer Networking	Page 15	Questions 24 to 27
Part C	Computer Programming	Page 17	Questions 28 to 31
Part D	Multimedia Technology	Page 21	Questions 32 to 35

For the sub-section chosen, attempt three questions

the <u>first two</u> questions and <u>either</u> the third question <u>or</u> the fourth question.

[Turn over

SECTION III

Part A—Artificial Intelligence

Marks

Attempt Question 20 and Question 21
and <u>either</u> Question 22 <u>or</u> Question 23

20. (a) MYCIN is an expert system which is used for medical diagnosis. It has been in use for over three decades and during this time it has been continually improved.

    (i) Describe **two** advances in **hardware** which have contributed to its improvement over this time.

    (ii) Describe **one** legal implication of using such expert systems and suggest how a good explanatory interface within an expert system could help to prevent such problems.

    (iii) Suggest **two** reasons why expert systems such as MYCIN are useful even though there may be several human experts in various medical centres around the world.

6

(b) Knowledge acquisition is an important stage in the development of an expert system. Explain why knowledge acquisition is an *iterative* process.

2

(c) Expert systems is one area of current artificial intelligence (AI) research. Others include *natural language processing* and *computer vision*. Suggest **two** reasons why there is such a large number of areas for research within the field of AI.

2

Marks

SECTION III

Part A—Artificial Intelligence (continued)

21. The following knowledge base summarises the management structure of a small company.

```
1   is_manager_of(friedland,bennett)        Friedland is Bennett's
                                            manager
2   is_manager_of(friedland,brown)
3   is_manager_of(friedland,everson)
4   is_manager_of(grainger,friedland)
5   is_manager_of(grainger,hill)
6   is_manager_of(hill,backley)
7   is_manager_of(hill,foster)

8   male(everson)
9   male(foster)
10  male(grainger)
11  male(hill)

12  female(X) if                            X is female if X is
    not male(X)                             not male

13  boss(X,Y) if                            X is Y's boss if X is
    is_manager_of(X,Y)                      Y's manager

14  boss(X,Y) if                            X is Y's boss if
    is_manager_of(X,Z)and                   X is the manager of Z and
    boss(Z,Y)                               Z is Y's boss
```

(a) (i) What would be the result of the following query?

?male(macdonald)

(ii) In terms of this knowledge base, what problem is there with this result?　　　　2

(b) Trace the solution to the query:

?female(friedland)　　　　2

(c) Write a complex query to find out which female employees have Grainger as their boss.　　　　2

(d) Two people are in the same department if they have the same immediate manager. Design a rule to show this.　　　　2

(e) (i) Explain why the rules in lines 13 and 14 are both required.

(ii) Why must they appear in the order shown?　　　　2

[Turn over

Marks

SECTION III

Part A—Artificial Intelligence (continued)

Attempt **either** Question 22 **or** Question 23

22. (a) Give **two** reasons why simple game playing was an important part of early artificial intelligence research. **2**

(b) A computer has been programmed to play noughts and crosses against a human opponent. The human opponent does not know whether he is playing against a computer or another human. He has been asked to work out which it is.

Why would it be difficult for a human player to decide whether he was playing against a computer or another human? **2**

(c) A robot is being programmed to solve a jigsaw puzzle using computer vision techniques.

   (i) Describe **two** difficulties when using computer vision in this context.

   (ii) Suggest how the use of a simple *heuristic* may be applied to the computer vision algorithm to solve a jigsaw puzzle. **4**

(d) State clearly how research into *pattern matching* and *parallel processing* may assist in the development of intelligent robots. **2**

23. (a) Databases and knowledge bases are both used to store information. Describe **two** ways in which they differ. **2**

(b) Give **one** reason why the knowledge base and inference engine are separated in the traditional architecture of an expert system shell. **1**

(c) A *domain expert* provides the knowledge which is stored in an expert system. Name **one** other person who is involved in creating an expert system and **describe** the role of this person. **1**

(d) In many situations human experts cannot be precise about the advice that they give. They may only be able to say that their advice is very likely to be correct in a particular situation.

   (i) Describe a feature of an expert system that could help to model this type of advice.

   (ii) Describe how this feature might be used in a particular situation. **2**

(e) Advice from an expert system can be arrived at by using either *forward chaining* or *backward chaining*.

   (i) Using a syntax with which you are familiar, give an example of a forward chaining rule and a backward chaining rule.

   (ii) For what type of problem is forward chaining best suited?

   (iii) To what type of problem is backward chaining best suited? **4**

[END OF SECTION III PART A]

SECTION III

Part B—Computer Networking

Marks

Attempt Question 24 and Question 25
and <u>either</u> Question 26 <u>or</u> Question 27

24. A large insurance company makes extensive use of the Internet and e-mail. The company also has computer-based networked information systems and its own intranet. Some of the company's staff have access to the entire network from home using a dial-up connection.

   (a) The company has used the *client-server* networking model rather than the *peer-to-peer* model when designing its network.

      (i) Explain the terms "peer-to-peer" and "client-server".

      (ii) Give **two** reasons why it has chosen the client-server model.   4

   (b) Suggest **two** reasons why access to the company's network is slower from home than it is from the office.   2

   (c) The IT Manager is worried that the company's network might be broken into by unauthorised people.

      Describe **two** ways a *firewall* could prevent unauthorised access.   2

   (d) The dial-up server offers a "callback" facility. When an employee dials from home, the dial-up server checks their user name and password, terminates the connection and then re-establishes the link to the employee's home number.

      Give **two** reasons why this feature is used in addition to the firewall.   2

25. A business has several large offices, one in each of the main capital cities of Europe. Each office has a local area network (LAN) of desktop computers. The company now wishes to connect all of the offices to one another, so that any computer in one office can access data which is stored on the server of another office. The TCP/IP stack is used on all of the computers.

   (a) (i) What **device** is necessary to connect the LANs?

      (ii) Give **one** reason for your choice.   2

   (b) Describe the steps involved in the transfer of files between computers using the TCP/IP protocol.   2

   (c) One of the company's LANs provides multimedia CD-ROM sharing. State, with reasons, **two** requirements of the LAN for this to operate satisfactorily.   2

   (d) The business makes heavy use of printed output. Describe **two** functions provided by a *print server* to control printing.   2

   (e) Explain how the use of TCP/IP has led to the development and growth of *intranets*.   2

[Turn over

Marks

SECTION III

Part B—Computer Networking (continued)

Answer either Question 26 or Question 27

26. (a) It is claimed that: "computer networks create information rich and information poor individuals or societies".

    Explain what is meant by this statement. **2**

    (b) When downloading or using information from another country, a user may accidently break the law. Why might this cause difficulties for legal authorities across the world? **2**

    (c) A method called the Domain Name System is used to construct Internet addresses. A URL is of the form:

    protocol: // host_address/resource name

    For each part of the URL:

    (i) describe its purpose, and

    (ii) give an example from an actual URL. **3**

    (d) A major step forward in the development of the Internet was the development of *packet switching* as a data transmission method.

    (i) State **one** other data transmission method.

    (ii) Describe **two** advantages of packet switching when compared to your answer to (i). **3**

27. A team of fashion designers work in an office with computers which are connected to a local area network. They also have access to the World Wide Web. Each member of the team has a laptop and a digital camera which they use when working away from their main office.

    (a) (i) Name **one** item of hardware and **one** item of software which would be needed to allow communication between the laptops and the office server.

    (ii) Describe **two** tasks that the item of **software** would carry out. **3**

    (b) The team also uses video conferencing to share ideas and information when meetings in the office are not possible.

    (i) Describe **two** facilities which video conferencing makes available.

    (ii) Security is an important consideration for this company. How can the company ensure that a video conference is secure? **3**

    (c) (i) Name a file format which is suitable for transmitting photographs over a typical Internet link.

    (ii) Describe **two** features of this file format which make it suitable for this purpose. **2**

    (d) The fashion house transmits its designs over a wide-area-network (WAN) which conforms to the Open Systems Interconnection (OSI) model.

    Name and describe **two** layers of the OSI model. **2**

[END OF SECTION III PART B]

SECTION III

Part C—Computer Programming

Marks

**Attempt Question 28 and Question 29
and <u>either</u> Question 30 <u>or</u> Question 31**

28. When a computer receives an *interrupt* signal from a peripheral requiring attention, it saves the address of the instruction that it is currently processing by *pushing* it onto a *stack*. When it has dealt with the peripheral, it *pops* the saved address for the previous task from the stack and carries on from where it stopped.

    (*a*) What type of data structure will be used to implement the stack? Your answer should state the **full** data type of the data structure. **1**

    (*b*) What **two** items of data must the program hold if it is to be able to use the stack? **2**

    (*c*) Describe the process of *pushing* an item onto a stack. You may use a diagram to illustrate your answer. **3**

    (*d*) Another part of the software deals with holding jobs in a print queue. Jobs in this queue are carried out in order of priority. This is determined by the two digit job number allocated to the document to be printed. Jobs are held in a sorted list. Any new jobs are added to the list and the list is then re-ordered.

    Example:

    Old list: 13, 27, 39, 42

    Job number 13 is sent to the printer and the queue manager receives a new job from a user (31).

    Unsorted list: 27, 39, 42, 31
    New list: 27, 31, 39, 42

    (i) Describe, using pseudocode or otherwise, **one** method of sorting the list:

    27, 39, 42, 31.

    (ii) Describe the efficiency of your sorting algorithm in terms of the number of comparisons and memory use. **4**

[Turn over

Marks

SECTION III

Part C—Computer Programming (continued)

29. A wages program is to read an alphabetical list of names and the number of hours worked from a text file. Each person's data is to be held as a pair on a single line in the file. Before the weekly wage is calculated, the data is to be read into two parallel one-dimensional arrays. The hourly rate will be held in a variable called **rate**. The calculated wages are stored in a third array before being output to the printer.

(a) The developers are worried about generating a *run-time error* whilst reading the data from the file.

   (i) Describe a "run-time error" that could occur at this stage.

  (ii) Describe a programming method, or language structure, that could be used to detect this error and so prevent the program from crashing.   **3**

(b) Using pseudocode or another suitable form, show how the data is read into arrays from the text file.   **3**

(c) The wages program will be implemented in a high level language. High level language programs need to be translated using either an interpreter or a compiler.

Use a loop construct from a language with which you are familiar to compare the efficiency of translation and execution using a compiler and an interpreter.   **2**

(d) When an employee leaves the company, the employee's data is removed from the wages list. Describe, using an algorithm or other method, how a data pair at a given position in the arrays could be removed so that when the arrays are output back to the file there will be no blank lines.

It may be assumed that the item has been found and is held in an appropriate variable.   **2**

Marks

SECTION III

Part C—Computer Programming (continued)

Answer either Question 30 or Question 31

30. Below is an extract from the datafile used by the Cree Valley Cookery Club to hold details of their 128 members. It holds the Membership Number, Member Name, Membership Class and Favourite Recipe of each member.

Membership Number	Member Name	Membership Class	Favourite Recipe
112	Seawright, D	Full	Game Pie
113	Ramsay, R	Student	Pork Casserole
114	Edeling, M	Full	Chocolate Cake
115	Lloyd, C	Full	Mushroom Pastry
116	Carrick, E	Full	Grilled Swordfish

(a) The software will report how many members of a given Membership Class are in the file. Name the standard algorithm that is used in this part of the software. 1

During the implementation phase, programming teams refer to a detailed algorithm of the software produced by the design team. After the code is written, a *dry run* is carried out followed by *component testing* and testing of the finished product.

(b) What is the purpose of a "dry run" and how is it carried out? 1

(c) Give **two** reasons for carrying out "component testing". 2

(d) Explain how *trace tables* and *break points* are used in the testing process. 2

The software searches the file on any of the fields and displays the first record it finds that matches the search item.

(e) A member's details are found with a simple *linear search* on the Member Name.

(i) The time taken to access an individual record in the file is 0·05 seconds. How long would it take to find that the name "Cobbold, T" is **not** in the file?

(ii) If a *binary search* was used on a file of this size, how long would it take to reach the same result for "Cobbold, T"? Show all your working.

(iii) Explain why a *binary search* would not work on the list of records shown above. 4

[Turn over

Marks

SECTION III

Part C—Computer Programming (continued)

31. When a product code is scanned at a stock warehouse, the scanning software performs a validity check by calculating a check digit.

The first ten digits are added together and then divided by nine. The check digit is the **remainder** after dividing by nine.

(a) The code to calculate the check digit is saved as a *library function*. What is a library function?　　**1**

(b) The function uses a loop to calculate the check digit. Using pseudocode, or another design notation, **fully** describe the check digit function.　　**3**

(c) Explain the use of a *debugger* at the implementation stage.　　**2**

(d) The product codes and the number of items of each product are kept in two parallel arrays as shown below.

Product Code	3542568390	8745359826	2575389925	6541212003	7437645426	8734521892

Number	150	160	145	110	250	150

(i) Explain **two** difficulties that could result from a solution using parallel arrays.

(ii) Describe an alternative to using parallel arrays for the above problem and show how this would solve one of the problems identified in (i) above.　　**4**

[END OF SECTION III PART C]

SECTION III

Part D—Multimedia Technology

Marks

**Attempt Question 32 and Question 33
and <u>either</u> Question 34 <u>or</u> Question 35**

32. When creating a multimedia presentation, many different types of software could be used.

    (a) (i) Describe **two** different types of **authoring software** which could be used to create a multimedia presentation.

    (ii) Describe **one** advantage of each type. **4**

    (b) Both hardware and software for multimedia are subject to international standards.

    (i) Explain the purpose of MPC standards.

    (ii) Name **one** minimum **hardware** requirement for an MPC computer and explain why your choice is a necessary feature of a multimedia computer. **3**

    (c) The World Wide Web allows interactive multimedia presentations to be viewed around the world. It allows users to download multimedia elements such as graphics and videos.

    (i) How have *hypertext* systems contributed to the development of the World Wide Web?

    (ii) Explain the need for *compression* when storing multimedia elements.

    (iii) Explain the legal implications of downloading media elements from the World Wide Web. **3**

[Turn over

SECTION III

Part D—Multimedia Technology (continued)

Marks

33. A graphic artist uses *image processing* software to produce various artwork pieces. The artist has decided to use a bit-mapped package.

   (*a*) The image processing software allows the artist to edit individual pixels.

       Describe **three** other features of this type of image processing software.   **3**

   (*b*) (i) Identify **two** file formats the artist could use to save her artwork.

       (ii) Describe **one** advantage of **each** of your formats.   **3**

   (*c*) The artist wants to store her artwork to allow it to be distributed to prospective buyers.

       (i) What backing storage medium would you recommend? Give **two** reasons for your choice.

       (ii) A buyer has the appropriate backing storage device to read the medium from (i).

          Describe **two** possible problems a buyer could still have when trying to access the artwork.   **4**

Marks

SECTION III

Part D—Multimedia Technology (continued)

Answer either Question 34 or Question 35

34. A company produces videos for various occasions such as parties and weddings. They use standard analogue video cameras. The company wishes to use a computer with video editing software to edit the videos captured by the camera.

    (a) (i) Explain how the frames stored in the camera can be captured and saved to backing storage. Your answer should include relevant hardware and software at each stage.

    (ii) How could a **digital** video camera benefit the company in this situation?   4

    (b) Most videos are captured at 25 frames per second.

    (i) State **one** advantage and **one** disadvantage of capturing at 10 frames per second compared with capturing at 25 frames per second.

    (ii) State **one** advantage and **one** disadvantage of capturing at 50 frames per second compared with capturing at 25 frames per second.   2

    (c) (i) Describe **two** features of video editing software.

    (ii) Describe **two hardware** requirements of a computer system which is to be used for video editing.

    Your answer must include appropriate units.   4

35. Sound and animation are two examples of multimedia elements that can be used when creating presentations and web pages. Various file formats and compression techniques are commonly used when storing these elements.

    (a) Explain the difference between *lossy* and *lossless compression*.   1

    (b) Scanners are now a common feature of multimedia technology to capture images and text.

    Explain, in detail, how a scanner could be used to capture text as a text file.   3

    (c) Describe **two** different file formats which could be used to save text documents.   2

    (d) Many multimedia presentations use sound for music, voice playback and sound effects.

    (i) Explain the difference between *sampled* sound and *synthesised* sound.

    (ii) Describe **two** functions of a basic sound card.   4

[END OF SECTION III PART D]

[END OF QUESTION PAPER]

[BLANK PAGE]

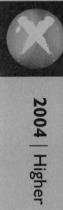

[BLANK PAGE]

X017/301

| NATIONAL QUALIFICATIONS 2004 | MONDAY, 31 MAY 1.00 PM – 3.30 PM | COMPUTING HIGHER |

Attempt **all** questions in Section I.

Attempt **four** questions in Section II

Question 14 and Question 15
and **either** Question 16 **or** Question 17
and **either** Question 18 **or** Question 19

Attempt **one** sub-section of Section III.

Part A	Artificial Intelligence	Page 14	Questions 20 to 23
Part B	Computer Networking	Page 18	Questions 24 to 27
Part C	Computer Programming	Page 20	Questions 28 to 31
Part D	Multimedia Technology	Page 24	Questions 32 to 35

For the sub-section chosen, attempt **three** questions.

The **first two** questions and **either** the third question **or** the fourth question.

Read all questions carefully.

Do not write on the question paper.

Write as neatly as possible.

SCOTTISH
QUALIFICATIONS
AUTHORITY

SECTION I

Attempt all questions in this section

Marks

1. A computer company named Complete Computers has used a drawing application to create the company logo shown below.

    The graphic is stored in a *vector graphics* format.

    (*a*) Explain how "vector graphics" are stored.   1

    (*b*) Write down a possible vector graphic representation for the rectangle in the logo shown above.   1

2. A microcomputer has a 24 bit address bus and a 16 bit data bus. It also has a control bus.

    (*a*) Describe how the operation of the control bus differs from that of the address and data buses.   2

    (*b*) Calculate the number of addresses that are available to the microcomputer.   1

3. State **two** characteristics of a laser printer which will affect the speed of printing.   2

4. State **two** functions of an interface.   2

5. In computer systems, large numbers are stored using *floating point representation*.

    State the effect of increasing the number of bits used to store:

    (i) the mantissa;

    (ii) the exponent.   2

6. The operating system includes functions such as Input/Output, File Management and Memory Management.

    When loading a file from a floppy disk:

    (*a*) describe **one** task that the Input/Output function would perform when loading the file;   1

    (*b*) describe **one** task that the Memory Management function would perform when loading the file.   1

Marks

SECTION I (continued)

7. Data integrity describes the accuracy of data when being processed or transmitted.

    (*a*) Describe **one** method of ensuring data integrity.   1

    (*b*) Describe how measures taken to ensure data integrity may affect overall system performance.   1

8. A program processes the details of members of a golf club. It uses *local variables* and *global variables*. The program stores each member's name and subscription payment.

    (*a*) State what is meant by a "global variable".   1

    (*b*) State **one** method of storing all the members' annual subscription payments.   1

9. A computer program is used to perform a multiple-choice survey of secondary pupils' opinions on certain topics. The program asks for the pupil's gender and age. All inputs are validated.

    (*a*) (i) State the **three** types of test data that are normally used to test programs.

    (ii) Give an example for **each** one that could be used to test the age validation part of the above program.   3

    (*b*) The program then analyses the data by finding how many females responded to the survey. Which one of the following algorithms would be required to do this?

    (i) Input validation

    (ii) Finding maximum

    (iii) Counting occurrences

    (iv) Linear search

    (v) Finding minimum   1

10. Maintenance of a program is greatly aided by its *readability*. State **two** methods that can be used to make a program readable.   2

11. The software development process begins with analysis and then moves on to design.

    (*a*) State **two** techniques which may be used at the analysis stage.   1

    (*b*) State the purpose of the design stage.   1

    (*c*) **Describe** a suitable method of representing a program design. It is not sufficient to simply name the method.   1

SECTION I (continued)

12.   Parameters can be *passed by reference* or *passed by value*.

   (*a*)   Explain what is meant by a parameter.   1

   (*b*)   Explain what is meant by "passed by reference".   1

13.   Programmers often use *module libraries* when writing programs.

   Give **two** reasons why a "module library" would be used during the development of software.   2

[END OF SECTION I]

Marks

SECTION II

Attempt FOUR questions in this section

Question 14 and Question 15
and _either_ Question 16 _or_ Question 17
and _either_ Question 18 _or_ Question 19

14. A railway company is planning a new way to collect fares. Regular passengers will have an identification swipe card that will be passed through a reader at the start of each journey. The data collected will be transmitted from the card reader to the head office computer for processing.

    The billing program will calculate the cheapest fare and produce monthly accounts for each passenger.

    (a) Which one of the following algorithms is most likely to be used in the billing program?

    　　(i) Linear search

    　　(ii) Finding maximum

    　　(iii) Finding minimum

    　　(iv) Counting occurrences　　　　　　　　　　　　　　　　　　1

    (b) (i) Explain why it is important to check the design of an algorithm **before** coding.

    　　(ii) Describe **one** method of checking the design of an algorithm.　　2

    (c) When the program is implemented the programming team find that it does not work. Two software development tools that the team use are *error tracing* and *error reporting*.

    　　Describe how the team could use **each** of these tools to fix the program.　　2

    (d) At the end of each billing period, discounts will be given to passengers based on the number of miles travelled. The table below shows the discounts.

Miles Travelled	Discount
Over 750	15%
501–750	10%
251–500	5%
250 or less	0%

    Using a design notation with which you are familiar, demonstrate how a *selection control structure* could be used to implement the discount rates and calculate the discounted bill.　　3

    (e) Information on passenger travel is used by various departments of the company for marketing and planning. All data is saved using a *standard data format*.

    　　(i) What is meant by a "standard data format"?

    　　(ii) Why is it important to use a standard data format in this situation?　　2

Marks

SECTION II (continued)

15. The Brown family has five standalone desktop computers in their household. The family wants to connect them to form a small local area network.

    (*a*) (i) What specific hardware **and** software will need to be present in the desktop computers in order for them to be connected to the network?

        (ii) Draw a labelled diagram of a suitable topology for this network.   **3**

    (*b*) Once the network has been set up, the three children in the family and their friends amuse themselves by playing games against each other across the network. The children feel that the system performance could be better.

        Suggest, **with reasons**, **two** hardware improvements that could be made to improve performance.   **2**

    (*c*) The Brown family accesses the Internet regularly, saving World Wide Web pages and downloading files.

        (i) Name **one** type of utility program that may be used while downloading files **and** explain why it is used here.

        (ii) After a period of time, the Brown family notices a decrease in system performance.

            Name **one** type of utility program that may be used to improve system performance **and** explain why it is used here.   **3**

    (*d*) The eldest Brown child wants to create his own computer games. He chooses an *event-driven* language to create his games.

        Give **two** reasons why an "event-driven" language is suitable for this task.   **2**

Marks

SECTION II (continued)

Attempt either Question 16 or Question 17

16. Shelby's coaches has advertised for new bus drivers. Applicants are interviewed if they:

    - are over 25 years old

    - hold a current driver's licence

    - have 3 years driving experience.

The program will work out if the applicant is allowed an interview.

The entry for one applicant is shown below.

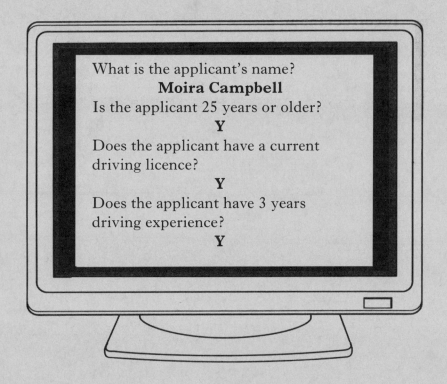

The program uses the following steps.

```
For each applicant

    Step 1 - Get and store input from user

    Step 2 - Work out if applicant is acceptable for
             an interview

End loop
```

(a) Step 1 requires four variables. **Three** of these variables are parameters passed to Step 2.

    (i) Would they be passed by reference or value? Justify your answer.

    (ii) Identify one other variable which must be used in Step 2 and state its data type.

2

Marks

SECTION II (continued)

16. (continued)

(*b*) The next applicant's entry is shown below.

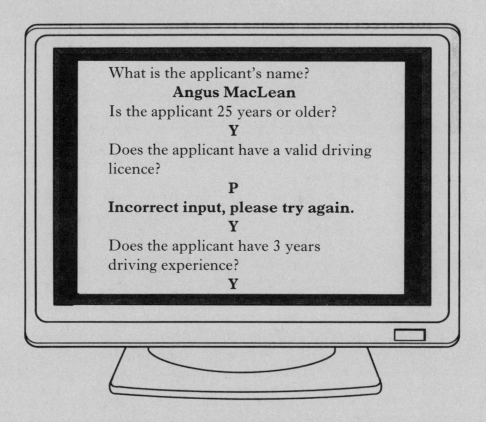

What is the applicant's name?
Angus MacLean
Is the applicant 25 years or older?
Y
Does the applicant have a valid driving licence?
P
Incorrect input, please try again.
Y
Does the applicant have 3 years driving experience?
Y

Describe how the program could ensure that the Driving Licence input is correct. You may use an appropriate design notation.   **3**

(*c*) For Step 2, the program will require a *complex condition* and a *control structure*. Using an appropriate design notation, show how these structures could be used to determine whether an applicant should be interviewed.   **2**

(*d*) Describe **one** situation where the program may require *adaptive maintenance*.   **1**

(*e*) A procedural language or a declarative language could be used to create the program. Which language would you choose? Give **two** reasons to justify your choice.   **2**

Marks

SECTION II (continued)

17. A client has employed a software house to create a program which will construct reports for its customers.

   (a) The design stage is one of the stages within the software development process.

      (i) Name **one** document which must be ready for the design team before they begin this stage.

      (ii) Describe **two** guidelines the design team could follow when designing the user interface.   3

   (b) The software house has developed a *modular program*.

      (i) Explain what is meant by a "modular program".

      (ii) Describe **two** techniques which may be used when creating a modular program.   3

   (c) The testing stage involves both the software house and the client company.

      Explain why **both** parties are required at this stage.   2

   (d) Identify **two** hardware requirements the software house might define and explain why these are important for the program that is being developed.   2

                                                                        [Turn over

Marks

SECTION II (continued)

Attempt either Question 18 or Question 19

18. A hospital uses a digital camera to obtain pictures of staff for identity cards.

A database of these pictures is held in a central server that senior staff and security staff can access across the hospital's local area network.

(*a*) The hospital could have used a general purpose database to store the pictures or it could have had a completely new program created just for this purpose.

Which would you recommend? Give reasons for your answer. 2

(*b*) The pictures are 2400 by 800 pixels and use 16-bit greyscale.

Calculate the amount of memory required to store a single scanned image.

Show all of your working. 2

(*c*) The hospital has 400 members of staff. What backing storage device would you recommend for storing the pictures? Justify your answer. 1

(*d*) The hospital has decided that only security staff should be able to access the database of pictures.

   (i) Describe **two** methods that could be used to restrict access.

   (ii) Which method would you recommend? Explain your choice. 3

(*e*) The local health authority has decided to use this program in all of its hospitals. Some of the hospitals use different computer systems. Describe **two** programming techniques that could have been used when writing the program which would have made it easier to transfer the program to different computer systems. 2

Marks

SECTION II (continued)

19. KoolSoundz is a sound-effects program that allows the user to add a variety of sounds to a computer. These are activated by a key press or by common actions, such as ejecting a disk.

    (*a*) This program may be useful to certain types of user, other than just providing amusement.

    Describe a situation where the software could be useful to the user.   **1**

    (*b*) The individual sounds are held as a group of integers. Two methods of storing an integer number are *signed bit* and *two's complement*.

    (i) Using 8 bits, show how the number **–120** is represented by **each** of these methods.

    (ii) State **two** reasons why "two's complement" is better than "signed bit" for storing negative numbers.   **4**

    (*c*) Explain the stages of the *fetch-execute cycle*.

    Your answer should make reference to the buses used at each stage.   **3**

    (*d*) The advertising states that the latest version of the KoolSoundz program is only guaranteed to run on computers using processors from one manufacturer.

    (i) Explain why the software may not run on machines using a processor from another manufacturer.

    (ii) Describe **one** solution that will allow computers with other types of processor to use this software product.   **2**

    [*END OF SECTION II*]

[Turn over

[BLANK PAGE]

SECTION III

Attempt ONE sub-section of Section III

Part A   Artificial Intelligence   Page 14   Questions 20 to 23
Part B   Computer Networking   Page 18   Questions 24 to 27
Part C   Computer Programming   Page 20   Questions 28 to 31
Part D   Multimedia Technology   Page 24   Questions 32 to 35

For the sub-section chosen, attempt three questions

the <u>first two</u> questions and <u>either</u> the third question <u>or</u> the fourth question.

[Turn over

Marks

SECTION III

Part A—Artificial Intelligence

**Attempt Question 20 and Question 21
and <u>either</u> Question 22 <u>or</u> Question 23**

20. A team of zoologists is studying insect life in a part of the Rainforest. The team is using a program to help store information about the diets of the most common ants and beetles in this remote area.

Some of the information held in the program is shown below.

```
1   ant(cropper black)              (the "cropper" ant is black)
2   ant(skullhead black)
3   ant(chipper red)
4   ant(bosun blue)
5   ant(borer red)

6   beetle(hopper green)            (the "hopper" beetle is green)
7   beetle(flagman blue)
8   beetle(crawler red)
9   beetle(grinder yellow)

10  plant(wood)                     ("wood" is a plant)
11  plant(leaves)
12  plant(fruit)

13  eats(cropper leaves)            (the "cropper" eats leaves)
14  eats(skullhead chipper)
15  eats(chipper wood)
16  eats(bosun leaves)
17  eats(borer grinder)
18  eats(flagman fruit)
19  eats(crawler grinder)
20  eats(grinder grass)
```

```
21  herbivore(X) :- eats(X Y)  and      (X is a herbivore if it
                    plant(Y)             eats Y and Y is a plant)
```

```
22  carnivore(X) :- eats(X Y)  and      (X is a carnivore if it
                    not(plant(Y))        eats Y and Y is not a
                                         plant)
```

Marks

SECTION III

Part A—Artificial Intelligence (continued)

20. **(continued)**

   (a) (i) What is the answer to the following query?

   ```
   ? beetle(grinder X)
   ```

   (ii) How many solutions would be found to the following query?

   ```
   ? beetle(X Y)
   ```
   2

   (b) Show how the system finds the solution to the following query.

   ```
   ? carnivore(grinder)
   ```

   Use the line numbers given in the program to help your explanation. 3

   (c) (i) What did you find unusual about your answer to part (b)?

   (ii) Why did this happen? 2

   (d) The use of an underscore in a query means that you "don't care" about that part of the query. It can have any value.

   What solution(s) would result from the following query?

   ```
   ? beetle( _ black)
   ```
   1

   (e) The crawler beetle is a cannibal since it eats other beetles.

   Write a rule that will define a "cannibal" as a beetle that will eat other beetles. 2

21. An expert system is being developed by a company to help with installing and configuring networks. Information about all the most common errors encountered during the installation and testing of network systems is to be entered into the expert system by a team of programmers.

   (a) Name and describe the **three** main components of an expert system. 3

   (b) The company has to choose between using a *declarative language* or an *expert system shell* in the creation of the system.

   Describe **one** advantage and **one** disadvantage of choosing to implement the system in an expert system shell rather than using a declarative language. 2

   (c) The use of *certainty factors* was suggested to improve the software.

   (i) Use an example to explain the term "certainty factors".

   (ii) How might the use of certainty factors improve the software? 3

   (d) The use of *justification* features would aid network installers to diagnose network problems.

   Describe **two** ways that "justification" could be used in this situation. 2

Marks

SECTION III

Part A—Artificial Intelligence (continued)

Attempt either Question 22 or Question 23

22. One early area of study in Artificial Intelligence (AI) was in the field of game playing, eg, implementing games like chess.

    (a) Describe **two hardware** restrictions that the early AI developers faced when trying to create programs to play more complex games. Make clear the effect of **each** restriction on the application. 2

    (b) When trying to reach a goal state, many early systems relied upon the use of brute force search methods. Two methods are *depth-first* and *breadth-first*.

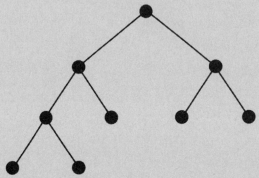

    (i) Copy the above diagram and label it to show how **both** the "breadth-first" and "depth-first" search methods find a solution.

    (ii) Explain why **one** of these search methods is more efficient in its use of memory than the other. 3

    (c) The application of a *heuristic* can improve the efficiency of the search.

    Explain how the use of a "heuristic" can improve the search time. 1

    (d) Early AI chess programs had difficulty in beating human opponents.

    Describe **two** ways that an AI program might improve its ability to beat human opponents. 2

    (e) A research team has been asked to design a voice recognition program for a computer game. The program must be able to recognise and respond to various commands spoken by the player.

    Describe **two** difficulties in the area of voice recognition that the team must try to overcome if the program is to be able to play the game effectively. 2

Marks

SECTION III

Part A—Artificial Intelligence (continued)

23. MarsCrawler is a mobile robot which has been designed to explore the surface of the planet Mars. It has a ROM-based operating system and specialised image processing software. It is also said to have in-built machine intelligence.

(*a*) State **two** advantages of having a **ROM-based**, instead of disk-based, operating system on the MarsCrawler.

2

(*b*) The MarsCrawler is often out of radio contact with the controllers and cannot relay pictures from its cameras. When this happens the robot must make decisions for itself until it can re-establish contact.

    (i) Describe **two** additional difficulties the image processing software might have in recognising objects on the surface of Mars when compared to the human controller.

    (ii) Describe a technique that could be used to help overcome **one** of these difficulties.

3

(*c*) The MarsCrawler will take readings from a number of sensors and use these readings to help it make decisions about safe routes as it explores the surface. It uses a *neural network* to choose the appropriate route.

    (i) Describe what is meant by the term "neural network".

    (ii) Describe how a neural network can be trained to show intelligent behaviour.

3

(*d*) Critics of the MarsCrawler system argue that no machine should be described as intelligent as "machines cannot be intelligent".

Do you agree with this criticism? Give **two** reasons for your answer.

2

[END OF SECTION III PART A]

Marks

SECTION III

Part B—Computer Networking

**Attempt Question 24 and Question 25
and <u>either</u> Question 26 <u>or</u> Question 27**

24. Two competing firms of lawyers are housed in the same building. The firms decide to merge to form one company. It is also decided to connect the local-area networks (LANs) of both firms together.

   (a) Additional hardware such as *repeaters* or *bridges* may be needed.

      (i) Describe the purpose of a "repeater".

      (ii) At what layer of the OSI model does a repeater operate?

      (iii) What does the use of a "bridge" imply about the two parts of the larger LAN?   3

   (b) Both the previous networks were peer-to-peer but the decision has been made to switch to a client-server network with a central fileserver. Describe the function of **two** additional servers which could be added to the network.   2

   (c) Give **one** advantage and **one** disadvantage of a client-server model.   2

   (d) Access to the World Wide Web will be provided. The company is concerned that unauthorised users may access its network. Explain how the company can protect the network.   1

   (e) The company decides to create an intranet which uses the TCP/IP protocol. Explain how the TCP/IP protocol controls the transfer of data between two computers on a network.   2

25. The growth of wide-area networks (WANs) can be attributed to a number of factors, some of which could be described as technical and others as economic.

   (a) Describe **two** technical factors which have influenced the growth of WANs.   2

   (b) A user's experience of a wide-area network will be affected by the *bandwidth* of their connection.

      (i) Explain what is meant by "bandwidth".

      (ii) Describe **two** techniques which can be used to make better use of the available bandwidth.   3

   (c) *Netiquette* is a code of conduct relating to the use of networks. Describe **two** examples of good "netiquette" that apply to e-mail.   2

   (d) Users will need to be able to delete and save files to their home directory but may not be allowed to change other files which they would need to access.

   How could a network administrator implement this?   1

   (e) The *application layer* and the *transport layer* are part of the OSI model. Describe the function of **both** of these layers.   2

Marks

SECTION III

Part B—Computer Networking (continued)

Answer either Question 26 or Question 27

26. A primary school has 15 standalone computers and a number of printers. The primary school wishes to create a local-area network.

    (a) Fibre optic cable and twisted pair cable have been suggested as possible transmission media. Which of these would you recommend? Give **two** reasons to support your answer.   2

    (b) A star topology and a bus topology are considered for the new network. Give **one** advantage and **one** disadvantage of a star topology over a bus topology.   2

    (c) The network will use a protocol called CSMA/CD because problems with collisions can occur.

       Explain how the CSMA/CD protocol operates.   2

    (d) A 5·5 Megabyte file is to be transferred from a server to a station. The transfer takes place at a 100 megabits per second.

       How long will the transfer of the file take?   2

    (e) During normal operation the performance is less than expected from the answer in part (d). Suggest **two** reasons for this slower performance.   2

27. A finance company based in a city centre office has decided to close the office and allow employees to work entirely from home. Instead of using its office based LAN, the company will have a website with information including facilities for prospective customers to e-mail them.

    (a) Describe **two** advantages for the company being Internet based rather than in an office with a LAN.   2

    (b) The employees could use a dial up connection from home to access the World Wide Web.

       State an alternative method of connection from home and give **one** advantage of this method over a dial up connection.   2

    (c) The company is concerned that confidential information contained in e-mails should be secure from unauthorised access. Describe a method of ensuring security of e-mails.   1

    (d) Name **two** international protocols for e-mail and downloading files and describe the purpose of each.   3

    (e) Some people are concerned that being able to buy goods and financial services on-line will widen the gap between rich and poor. Give **one** reason in support and **one** against this argument.   2

[END OF SECTION III PART B]

Marks

SECTION III

Part C—Computer Programming

**Attempt Question 28 and Question 29
and <u>either</u> Question 30 <u>or</u> Question 31**

28. A low level routine uses *stack* operations to process an input sequence of Scottish place names. Each storage location in the stack can hold text of any length. The stack is initially empty and the input sequence is as follows.

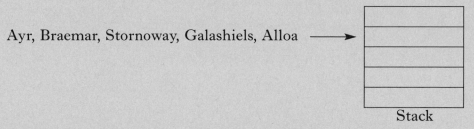

Ayr, Braemar, Stornoway, Galashiels, Alloa ⟶

Stack

Alloa is the first to enter the stack. An item is added to the stack by "*pushing*" and removed by "*popping*". After a "push push" operation, the contents of the stack are as follows

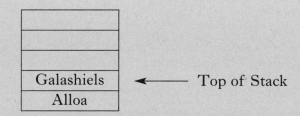

Galashiels ⟵ Top of Stack
Alloa

(a) Describe, using pseudocode or similar, the sequence of events involved in a "pop" operation.   3

(b) In designing the routine, what must the programmer do to prevent popping an item from an empty stack?   1

(c) Using the above list of Scottish place names, what would be the contents of the stack after the following sequence of actions? (Assume that the stack is empty to start with.)

    push, push, pop, push, push, pop, pop, push   2

(d) A list of 5000 place names is to be sorted into alphabetical order.

    (i) Name **two** sort routines which could be used for this.

    (ii) Compare these two routines in terms of use of memory and processor time.   4

Marks

SECTION III

Part C—Computer Programming (continued)

29. Each year, a museum carries out a check of all the items it owns. The museum uses a program to read a list of item names and associated dates of purchase into *parallel arrays*. The same data could be held in a *two dimensional array* or a *record structure*.

    (a) Explain what is meant by:

        (i) a "two dimensional array";

        (ii) a "record structure".   **2**

    (b) Compare the use of parallel arrays and records for storing the museum's data by considering their appropriateness for:

        (i) sorting on one of the elements;

        (ii) searching on a given criterion for related data.   **4**

    (c) Give an example to show when the use of a two dimensional array would be better than using parallel arrays. Explain why a two dimensional array is preferable for your example.   **2**

    (d) In many operations on arrays, loops may form part of the control structure. Describe how the translation and execution of a loop structure differs when an interpreter is used instead of a compiler.   **2**

[Turn over

Marks

SECTION III

Part C—Computer Programming (continued)

Answer either Question 30 or Question 31

30. A *queue* is a data structure used in programming. Queues have two pointers. In one programming environment, the front pointer (head) indicates the position of the front of the queue and the rear pointer (tail) indicates the position of the last item in the queue.

    (a) Explain why a queue is said to be a first-in-first-out structure.   1

    (b) Draw diagrams to illustrate the position of the pointers in the following queues:

       (i) the queue is empty;

       (ii) the queue contains two items.   2

    (c) Items have been removed from the queue. The rear pointer (tail) is at the end of the array.

       (i) What happens when another item is to be added to the queue?

       (ii) Draw a diagram to indicate the position of the pointers when this new item has been processed.   3

    (d) A keyboard buffer stores key presses in a queue in memory until the processor is free to accept them. Using a design notation with which you are familiar, and, using the definitions of the pointers given at the start of the question, write an algorithm to show what happens when the next key is pressed.   4

Marks

SECTION III

Part C—Computer Programming (continued)

31. There are two search techniques commonly in use. These are *linear search* and *binary search*. A programmer wants to write a search routine to find a restaurant in a local guide.

(a) Describe **two** requirements of a binary search that are not necessary for a linear search.　　　　**2**

(b) Using the following list, demonstrate the steps taken by a binary search algorithm when looking for "Farmhouse Feasts".

Castle Helena

Farmhouse Feasts

Fondue Pot

Joe and Pete's

La Potage

Soup and Sandwiches

Spaghetti and More

3

(c) Each time an order is taken, the chef at Farmhouse Feasts adds the name of the main course to the bottom of a list he is keeping to help him judge the popularity of the various dishes. The list is stored in an array.

　(i) Using a design notation with which you are familiar, show how the number of times a particular main course has been chosen can be found.

　(ii) By considering why this method of recording main courses chosen is inefficient, suggest how two parallel arrays could be used to record the number of times a main course has been chosen in a more efficient way.　　　　**5**

[END OF SECTION III PART C]

Marks

SECTION III

Part D—Multimedia Technology

Attempt Question 32 and Question 33
and either Question 34 or Question 35

32. *Computer based training* and *hypermedia* systems have influenced the development of multimedia. *Interactive video* has been a large part of this development.

    (*a*) (i) What is meant by "interactive video"?

    (ii) Give **one** reason why interactive video is a major part of computer based training.

    2

    (*b*) CDs and DVDs are the most common types of storage media for computer based training.

    (i) There are many types of CD, explain the difference between **two** of these.

    (ii) State **two** reasons why DVDs are now more popular than CDs for storing multimedia systems.

    3

    (*c*) (i) Give **one** advantage of using *hypertext* systems over *hypermedia* ones.

    (ii) Describe **two** possible problems which could occur when navigating "hypertext" systems.

    3

    (*d*) Describe **two** developments in computer hardware, other than backing storage, which have supported advances in multimedia. Justify your choices.

    2

33. A graphics design company produces logos for commercial firms. The company uses a bit-mapped image processing package to create the logos.

    (*a*) When creating an image the *resolution* and *bit depth* have to be specified.

    (i) Explain the terms "resolution" and "bit depth".

    (ii) Explain **one** advantage of lowering the resolution of an image.

    3

    (*b*) For some of the simple logos, the company reduced the bit depth from 16-bit to 8-bit and found no loss in the quality of the image. Why is this the case?

    2

    (*c*) (i) Name **two** file formats the company could use to save the final logo.

    (ii) Compare both formats and state **one** advantage of each over the other.

    3

    (*d*) The company has been considering creating animated logos for Web pages. Describe **two** problems that could arise when animated logos are being viewed on the World Wide Web.

    2

Marks

SECTION III

Part D—Multimedia Technology (continued)

Answer either Question 34 or Question 35

34. A travel agent uses a multimedia system within its stores to allow customers to view and find information about possible holidays.

    (a) An authoring language was used to develop the multimedia system.

        (i) Describe **two** features of an *icon-based* authoring language.

        (ii) Give **one** advantage to the **developers** of using a *script-based* authoring language.   **3**

    (b) The multimedia system allows the customers to view video clips of possible holidays. Describe **two** possible technical problems which may have occurred during the capture of the video clips onto the computer system.   **2**

    (c) (i) Explain why *compression* is necessary when storing video within a computer system.

        (ii) Describe **one** video standard which uses compression techniques.   **2**

    (d) Describe, in detail, how the video clips could be included. Your explanation should include a description of any hardware or software used at each of the input, process and output stages.   **3**

35. A standard operating system is to be upgraded to include multimedia features. For example, it will have a facility for recording sound.

    (a) Describe **two** other examples of multimedia features which might have been added to the operating system.   **2**

    (b) Describe **one** audio standard which could be used when storing the audio files for the operating system.   **2**

    (c) The operating system is to be developed to allow the user to record and edit sound.

        (i) Describe **two** possible functions of a sound card which could be used when recording sound.

        (ii) Describe **two** features of audio processing software which could be used to edit sound.

        (iii) Describe **two** ways the user could ensure minimum loss of quality when recording sound.   **6**

[END OF SECTION III PART D]

[END OF QUESTION PAPER]

[BLANK PAGE]

2005 | Old Arrangements

[BLANK PAGE]

X017/301

| NATIONAL QUALIFICATIONS 2005 | MONDAY, 30 MAY 1.00 PM – 3.30 PM | COMPUTING HIGHER |

Attempt **all** questions in Section I.

Attempt **four** questions in Section II

Question 19 and Question 20
and **either** Question 21 **or** Question 22
and **either** Question 23 **or** Question 24

Attempt **one** sub-section of Section III.

Part A	Artificial Intelligence	Page 10	Questions 25 to 28
Part B	Computer Networking	Page 14	Questions 29 to 32
Part C	Computer Programming	Page 18	Questions 33 to 36
Part D	Multimedia Technology	Page 22	Questions 37 to 40

For the sub-section chosen, attempt **three** questions.

The **first two** questions and **either** the third question **or** the fourth question.

Read all questions carefully.

Do not write on the question paper.

Write as neatly as possible.

SCOTTISH
QUALIFICATIONS
AUTHORITY

SECTION I

Marks

Attempt all questions in this section

1. Explain how ensuring data integrity can result in a decrease in system performance.

   1

2. (a) What is a buffer?

   1

   (b) Explain the function of a buffer within a printer interface.

   1

3. In floating point notation what defines

   (i) the range

   (ii) the precision or accuracy

   of the numbers stored?

   1

4. (i) Describe how graphics are stored using a vector package.

   (ii) Describe in detail how this graphic would be stored using a vector package.

   2

5. State **two** characteristics of event-driven languages.

   2

6. Name **two** different **types** of utility software.

   1

7. On your computer at home you have a word processor and at school you use a different word processing application. The default file formats used by each are not compatible.

   Name a standard file format that the file could be saved in to allow both applications to read the same file.

   1

8. Describe **two** advantages of using a scripting language within an application package.

   2

9. A network server may be dedicated to provide a certain service to the network.

   State **two** examples of services.

   1

10. Describe **two** ways in which increasing the amount of RAM can improve system performance.

   2

Marks

SECTION I (continued)

11. A *problem specification* is produced at the analysis stage of the software development cycle.

    What is the purpose of this document?   1

12. Name and describe **two** techniques used for extracting information at the analysis stage of the software development cycle.   2

13. An employee with a disability makes use of a specialised input device, however it does not work with a recently installed piece of software.

    What type of maintenance would be required to alter the software to accept this type of input device?

    Justify your answer.   1

14. Name and describe **two** design methodologies.   2

15. Describe **two** tasks that could be carried out at the design stage of the software development process.   2

16. A program is evaluated as **not** *fit for purpose*.

    What does this mean about the program?   1

17. What is the term used for a value which can be accessed from anywhere in a program?   1

18. An after school club requires a piece of software which will check whether children are able to join the club. One requirement is that the children must be 6 to 10 years old inclusive.

    (a) Suggest **three** suitable categories of test data that would be used to test the program.

    Explain your choices.   3

    (b) Write a complex condition that could be used to reject invalid ages.   1

    (c) A list of the surnames of the members of the club have to be stored.

    State a data structure and data type that could be used to store this list.   1

[END OF SECTION I]

[Turn over

Marks

SECTION II

Attempt FOUR questions in this section

Question 19 and Question 20
and either Question 21 or Question 22
and either Question 23 or Question 24

19. A group of students are working together to create a piece of software for a local playgroup.

    The lecturer tells them that the program must be *modular*.

    (a) State **two** benefits of writing the program in a "modular" way.   2

    (b) Name and describe **two** software development tools that the students may use when implementing and testing the program   2

    (c) Name and describe **two** items that will have to be given to the playgroup on completion of the software in addition to the actual program.   2

    (d) Internal commentary and meaningful procedure/variable names are common techniques used to make a program readable. Describe **two** additional techniques that the students could use to make their program more readable.   2

    (e) The students find several errors in the program. State **two** possible types of error that may have occurred. Use code from a programming environment with which you are familiar to illustrate one example of each type of error.   2

20. Peter runs a photography store. He develops and prints photographs in various formats.

    (a) He decides to offer a red eye removal service on all digital images.

    Would he use bit-mapped graphic or vector graphic software? Explain your answer.   1

    (b) An image is 4×6 inches, has a resolution of 800 dpi and each pixel can display 65536 different colours.

    Calculate the storage requirements for this image assuming no compression is used. Express your answer using suitable units.

    Show ALL working.   2

    (c) Customers now bring their image files into the shop on portable storage media. Peter has to be able to read the files from these different devices.

    (i) Name **two** such storage media.

    (ii) Choose the **one** which you would recommend and give a reason why.   2

    (d) Peter uses photographic quality paper on his colour inkjet printer. What **two** characteristics should the printer have? Justify your answers.   2

    (e) Clock speed and word size are both indicators of processor performance.

    (i) Name **two** methods of **measuring** processor performance.

    (ii) Describe each of the methods named in part (i).   3

Marks

SECTION II (continued)

Attempt either Question 21 or Question 22

21. A website has been created by a software house for a bank. A program has been written to count and record the number of times each page linked to the home page is visited or "hit".

Sample output from the program is shown below:

Home Page Hit Counter
New Accounts (1078 hits)
Stocks and Shares (1001 hits)
High Interest Accounts (2000 hits)

(a) The evaluation stage is part of the Software Development Process. Give **one** reason why this stage benefits:

   (i) the bank;

   (ii) the software house.   2

(b) One of the software house's aims is to ensure a *reliable* program.

   (i) Explain what the term "reliable" means.

   (ii) Describe **two** methods the software house could use to ensure that the program is reliable **before** the software is released.   3

(c) Using a design notation with which you are familiar, write an algorithm which would find the maximum number of hits for any page within the website.   3

(d) Bank employees also need to search and use other websites. This could cause **technical** problems for the bank's computers. For example, employees may find that Web pages take a long time to download.

Describe **one other** technical problem the bank could have and describe a possible solution.   2

[Turn over

Marks

SECTION II (continued)

22. A computer program to run the registration process at Dunwearie High School is being developed.

    (a) It is very important that the finished software is *robust*.

    Explain what the term "robust" means. **1**

    (b) The software uses parameters throughout. These are either *passed by reference* or *passed by value*.

       (i) Describe what is meant by the term "passed by reference".

       (ii) Describe what is meant by the term "passed by value".

       (iii) Explain an advantage of "passing by value" rather than "passing by reference" in a program wherever possible. **3**

    (c) Part of the program will take in a pupil's surname and find the **position** of the pupil in a list. If the pupil is not found it reports this as an error.

    Using a design notation with which you are familiar, describe the part of the program that finds the position of the pupil in the list and reports an error if the pupil is not found. **3**

    (d) A section of the code reads through the list of absences and causes a letter home to be automatically sent out if **one** of the following two facts is true:

       • the number of unexplained absences is greater than zero

       • there has been a query from staff about absence **and** the total absences is greater than 5

    Using a design notation with which you are familiar, describe the single complex condition that must be satisfied to trigger the sending of the letter. **3**

Marks

SECTION II (continued)

Attempt either Question 23 or Question 24

23. Joe is playing a game program on his computer. The processor in Joe's computer uses a 24-bit *data bus* and a 32-bit *address bus*. The computer has a USB *interface*.

(a) Calculate the maximum amount of memory which Joe's computer could address. **2**

(b) Describe **two** functions of an interface. **2**

(c) The game was created using a high level language.

Name **two** types of translators that would have been considered. Which would you recommend? Give **two** reasons for your answer. **3**

(d) A new highest score is to be written to the high score table. This is done by a *memory write* operation. Describe how a typical processor would carry out a "memory write" operation. Your answer should mention the buses used at each stage. **3**

24. A software development company has been asked to create a new operating system. Different programmers have been given responsibility for the creation of operating system functions such as memory management and the command language interpreter.

(a) Describe **two** features of the user interface that you would include so that a user will have an opportunity to prevent or correct mistakes. **2**

(b) The operating system will be written using a high level language. Suggest a **type** of high level language which could be used and give **two** reasons to support your answer. **2**

(c) Memory management will perform a number of tasks during the loading of a file. Describe **two** of these tasks. **2**

(d) System performance can be affected by a number of factors including the settings of certain peripherals and the ability to multitask.

Suggest **two** display settings that could be altered and describe how they would affect system performance. **2**

(e) Most modern operating systems allow the computer to have several programs resident in memory at the same time, sharing a single processor. This is called multitasking.

How would multitasking affect system performance? **2**

[END OF SECTION II]

[Turn over

[BLANK PAGE]

SECTION III

Attempt ONE sub-section of Section III

Part A	Artificial Intelligence	Page 10	Questions 25 to 28
Part B	Computer Networking	Page 14	Questions 29 to 32
Part C	Computer Programming	Page 18	Questions 33 to 36
Part D	Multimedia Technology	Page 22	Questions 37 to 40

For the sub-section chosen, attempt three questions

the first two questions and either the third question or the fourth question.

[Turn over

Marks

SECTION III

Part A—Artificial Intelligence

**Attempt Question 25 and Question 26
and <u>either</u> Question 27 <u>or</u> Question 28**

25. A school pupil has created a knowledge base to describe part of our solar system.

```
1. star(the_sun)              { The sun is a star.}

2. planet(the_earth)          { The earth is a planet.}
3. planet(saturn)
4. planet(neptune)

5. orbits(the_earth the_sun)
6. orbits(mars the_sun)
7. orbits(saturn the_sun)
8. orbits(titan saturn)
9. orbits(nereid neptune)

10.satellite(X Y) if          { X is a satellite of Y
   orbits(X Y)                  if X orbits Y.}

11.satellite(X Y) if
   orbits(X Z) and
   satellite(Z Y)
```

   (a) What would be the output from the following queries?

   (i) ?orbits(nereid X)

   (ii) ?planet(X) and orbits(Y X)   3

   (b) Assuming a depth-first search is used, explain how the program would find the solutions to the following query.

   ?satellite (titan B)   3

   (c) A moon is to be defined as an object that orbits a planet. Design a "moon_of" rule for use in the knowledge base.   2

   (d) All of the objects go round the sun and are therefore satellites of the sun.

   However, the query ?satellite(nereid the_sun) gives the answer "No".

   Explain why this happens.   1

   (e) Explain **one** problem that might be encountered when trying to extend the knowledge base to describe all known stars?   1

Marks

SECTION III

Part A—Artificial Intelligence (continued)

26. Valuable objects are found by people using metal detectors and by other activities such as digging their gardens. Such objects are the subject of the law in Scotland and a company has decided to provide legal advice using an expert system.

    (a) A lawyer is consulted to provide information for the expert system. Identify the role of the lawyer in the creation of an expert system.   1

    (b) An expert system has three components. One component is the knowledge base. Name and describe the **two** other components of an expert system.   2

    (c) The lawyer provides the following information:

        "If a found item has been reported to the authorities and the Crown does not claim ownership then the finder has legal ownership."

        Design a rule to represent this information. Your rule may use either forward or backward chaining.   2

    (d) Once all of the rules are entered the expert system must be tested. How will the system be tested and who will be involved?   2

    (e) The fully tested expert system is made available on the World Wide Web and a user follows the advice given to them. However, the advice is wrong because the law is different in their country. Explain whether the user can be held responsible for breaking the law.   1

    (f) The expert system could have been created using a procedural language. Give **one** reason in support of using a procedural language and one against.   2

[Turn over

Marks

SECTION III

Part A—Artificial Intelligence (continued)

Attempt either Question 27 or Question 28

27. Expert systems and neural networks are attempts to model human intelligence.

    (a) Describe **two** problems involved in the modelling of intelligence.　　2

    (b) In human intelligence, the ability to explain your reasoning is important. Suggest how an expert system and a neural network would perform in this respect.　　2

    (c) A new car has a navigation system which is able to find a route between the driver's start point and the destination.

       (i) The navigation system could use a depth-first search or a breadth-first search. Describe how each of these methods operates. (You may use a diagram to illustrate your answer.)　　2

       (ii) The navigation system has limited memory. Explain which search method should be used.　　2

       (iii) Describe how parallel processing could be applied to this problem.　　2

Marks

SECTION III

Part A—Artificial Intelligence (continued)

28. A hospital holds many text-based reports of patient interviews in a computerised database. They decide to introduce natural language processing to help with searching. The system does not use speech input or voice recognition of any kind.

    (*a*) (i) Describe what is meant by natural language processing.

        (ii) Describe **two** problems associated with natural language processing. **3**

    (*b*) A doctor wants to search for cases where pneumonia has been found. A database search using the word "pneumonia" alone would result in matches such as:

        "pneumonia cannot be excluded"
        "rule out pneumonia"
        "pneumonia was confirmed"

    The second result is not relevant. However a search using "pneumonia found" may not find the first and third results which are relevant.

        (i) Suggest a reason why a search system using natural language processing would be more efficient.

        (ii) Suggest **two** reasons why a natural language processing system based on medical terms would be more likely to be successful in its implementation than one based on everyday language. **3**

    (*c*) State **two** advances in hardware that have aided the development of natural language processing and **describe how** they have aided the development of natural language processing. **2**

    (*d*) The hospital also has a medical expert system which is used to give possible diagnoses of illnesses. More than one possible diagnosis is often given.

    Describe how the diagnoses could be placed in order with the most likely diagnosis placed first. **2**

[END OF SECTION III PART A]

Marks

SECTION III

Part B—Computer Networking

**Attempt Question 29 and Question 30
and <u>either</u> Question 31 <u>or</u> Question 32**

29. A group of students are planning to connect their computers together so that they can play *NetSpider*, a new multi-player network game.

    (a) The students could choose either a *client-server* or a *peer-to-peer* model for their network.

        (i) Explain the terms "client-server" and "peer-to-peer".

        (ii) Give **one** reason why the students should use a "client-server" model.   3

    Updates for the game are available from the game developer's website.

    The URL for the update is given as:

    www.WebGrafters.co.uk/updates/Spider.zip

    (b) Referring to the above URL, explain the following terms:

        (i) domain name

        (ii) resource name.   2

    (c) The update file is transferred using a browser operating the TCP/IP standard internet protocol.

        (i) Describe how the transfer takes place under TCP/IP.

        (ii) Name another standard protocol that might be used to transfer this file.   3

    (d) The data line used by the students to download the file is rated at 15 megabits per second.

        (i) If the size of the update file is 112 megabytes, how long will it take to download?

        (ii) Give **two** reasons why it might take longer to download the file in practice.   2

Marks

SECTION III

Part B—Computer Networking (continued)

30. Castle Ruth hospital holds a database of scans, x-rays and photographs of both common and rare conditions. The database is available on the hospital Local Area Network (LAN). It is proposed to share this information with a group of researchers at the local university. This could be achieved by providing a dial-up service or by connecting the university LAN to the hospital LAN.

    (a) (i) Name the item of hardware that would be required to connect the university LAN to the hospital LAN.

        (ii) What name is given to this type of combined network?

        (iii) Describe **one** advantage of combining the LANs rather than using a dial-up connection.   3

    (b) There are two servers on the hospital LAN. One of these is a fileserver holding the database described in part (a) as well as other user files belonging to staff.

        (i) Name **one** other type of server that might be on the network and describe its function.

        (ii) User files can be protected by using passwords and setting access rights.

            Describe **two** other methods that might be employed to ensure security of user files on the fileserver.   3

    (c) This network uses a protocol called *CSMA/CD*. Describe the operation of "CSMA/CD".   2

    (d) The hospital and university are 4 kilometres apart. The two networks are connected by a dedicated cable.

        Suggest a suitable type of cable. Give **two** reasons for your choice.   2

[Turn over

Marks

SECTION III

Part B—Computer Networking (continued)

Answer either Question 31 or Question 32

31. International Pencils is a multinational office supplies company with branch offices in seven European capital cities. These branch offices are connected by a wide-area network (WAN).

    (a) The company use the network for *video conferencing*.

       (i) Give **two** advantages to the company of using "video conferencing".

       (ii) State **two** items of hardware which would be required to implement "video conferencing".   3

    (b) The company network conforms to the Open Systems Interconnection (OSI) model. It uses the following devices as part of the network infrastructure:

       • repeaters
       • bridges
       • routers

       Each of these devices operates at a different layer of the OSI model.

       Choose **two** of the above devices.

       (i) For **each** device, name the layer of the OSI model at which it operates.

       (ii) Describe these two layers of the OSI model.   4

    (c) Explain why it is important that networks are designed using standard models, such as OSI.   1

    (d) Each device on the International Pencils European network has a unique **48-bit address**. This is known as a MAC address.

       (i) Explain why it is necessary for each device on the network to have a MAC address.

       (ii) What is the maximum number of possible MAC addresses?   2

Marks

SECTION III

Part B—Computer Networking (continued)

32. Fragrant Futures is a charity dedicated to preserving wildflowers and older varieties of herbs and fruits. It plans to build an education centre with over 100 networked computers. This will allow school parties to access a very large central database of plants and view video clips.

(*a*) Describe **two** different technological or economic advances that have made the creation of such a network possible.

2

(*b*) The topology of the network has not been chosen yet.

   (i) Describe a suitable topology for this network.

   (ii) Explain why your chosen topology is suited to this task.

2

(*c*) The database can be added to by registered users and is held on a server.

   (i) Explain why it is necessary for this network to have a backup strategy.

   (ii) Describe a suitable backup strategy and explain how it could be implemented.

     Your answer should make reference to hardware and software required.

3

(*d*) Data transmission on the network will either operate by *packet-switching* or *circuit-switching*.

   (i) Explain the term "circuit-switching".

   (ii) Describe **one** advantage of "packet-switching" over "circuit-switching" for this network.

   (iii) Describe **one** advantage of "circuit-switching" over "packet-switching" for this network.

3

[END OF SECTION III PART B]

Marks

SECTION III

Part C—Computer Programming

Attempt Question 33 and Question 34
and <u>either</u> Question 35 <u>or</u> Question 36

33. A program is being developed which will generate a list of 5 random integers between 1 and 25 inclusive. A value within this list is then to be searched for. Below is an example of one such list generated by the program:

    1   18   15   7   12

    Each number on the list must not occur more than once.

    (a) Describe **two** features of a text editor which will allow the code to be typed up quickly. **2**

    (b) Iteration control structures have to be used within the program when checking that the next random number generated is not already on the list.

       (i) Describe **two** ways an iterative control structure could be coded incorrectly.

       (ii) Describe how the efficiency of a program may be affected if an iterative control structure has been coded incorrectly. **3**

    (c) (i) What must happen to the list above before a binary search can take place?

       (ii) Using a design notation with which you are familiar, explain how a binary search works. You may use the list above in your answer. **4**

    (d) Give **one** example of a situation when a linear search would be more efficient than a binary one. **1**

Marks

SECTION III

Part C—Computer Programming (continued)

34. An exam board uses a program to process candidates details. An example of the data that must be processed is shown below:

Candidate name	Candidate number	Subject	Pass
John Smith	102	Mathematics	N
Aileen MacLean	103	English	Y
Mary Sinclair	104	Mathematics	Y
Aileen MacLean	103	History	Y

An appropriate data structure must be chosen to manage this data.

(a) Explain fully what is meant by a data structure.   1

(b) (i) Explain why a two-dimensional array would not be a good choice of data structure in this case.

   (ii) Suggest a **single** data structure for this problem and describe this data structure in full.   4

(c) The data is stored in a file. Describe **two** file operations which could be required by the program. Justify your answers.   2

(d) The program has to work out how many subjects each candidate has passed. Which standard algorithm would be required to do this?   1

(e) The data has to be sorted into candidate number order. Describe **one** sort algorithm which could be used. You may use a design notation with which you are familiar for your description.   2

[Turn over

Marks

SECTION III

Part C—Computer Programming (continued)

Answer <u>either</u> Question 35 <u>or</u> Question 36

35. A software house has developed a program to process data for an international fruit store.

   Below is a section of the list of data which has to be input and stored by the program:

Top of data list

apples
bananas
coconuts

bottom of data list

   (a) During the implementation stage, debugging is carried out.

   (i) What is meant by debugging?

   (ii) Describe **two** methods of debugging a program.   **3**

   (b) Describe **fully** what data structure could be used to store this data within the program.   **1**

   (c) One of the features of the program is to count how many times a certain fruit appears on the total list of fruits. Describe using pseudocode or otherwise how this could be achieved within the program.   **3**

   (d) The fruit store has now decided to use the program to process data for the quantities of fruit in stock. The program needs to input and process both fruit names and quantities. For example:

Name	Quantity
Bananas	506
Apples	390
Coconuts	73

   The software house has decided to use parallel one-dimensional arrays to store this data.

   (i) Describe one problem that might result from the use of parallel one-dimensional arrays.

   (ii) If the data has to be stored in quantity order, explain how the items are relocated when data for a new fruit is inserted into the list.   **3**

Marks

SECTION III

Part C—Computer Programming (continued)

36. Queues and stacks are frequently used within programs when dealing with lists.

(*a*)   (i)   Explain fully the difference between a stack and a queue.

(ii)   Name **two** pointers which could be used to implement a queue.   **3**

(*b*)   A list of subjects that can be studied at school is shown below. The list is stored in an array and some items have been removed from the array.

List position

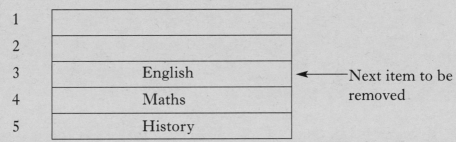

(i)   Describe what happens when Geography is added (pushed) to the list if a **queue** structure is being used.

You may use a diagram. Your answer should refer to any relevant pointers.

(ii)   Using the same list in (i) above show what would happen if a **stack** structure is being used.

You may use a diagram. Your answer should refer to any relevant pointers.   **3**

(*c*)   Indicate using pseudocode or otherwise how Geography is **pushed** onto the **stack**.   **2**

(*d*)   When unexpected events happen whilst a computer is running, the operating system can use *interrupts* to stop the processor carrying out its current task.

Would an operating system use a queue or stack to handle an interrupt? Justify your answer.   **2**

[END OF SECTION III PART C]

Marks

SECTION III

Part D—Multimedia Technology

**Attempt Question 37 and Question 38
and either Question 39 or Question 40**

37. Jamie wants to be able to put family photographs into a multimedia presentation; he has between 400 and 500 old photographs.

    (a) Jamie asks his relatives to provide audio comments for the photographs. Describe the steps he would follow to get these into his presentation. For each step you should include the relevant hardware **and** software.   **3**

    (b) Most computers available nowadays meet MPC standards.

    Why do we have MPC standards if most computers meet them?   **2**

    (c) The photographs are faded and torn. Jamie scans all his photographs.

       (i) Crop and sharpen are two features in image processing software which would help Jamie improve the images. Name and describe **two** other ways he could improve the image.

       (ii) The current MPC standard was specified several years ago. Give **two** amendments which could be made to it, giving reasons for your choices.   **4**

    (d) Explain why a script-based package would be better to develop the presentation than an icon-based package.   **1**

38. When designing a multimedia presentation a storyboard will often be used.

    (a) Give **two** reasons why a storyboard should be used to design the presentation.   **2**

    (b) Suggest **two** techniques a programmer may use to fully test the finished multimedia presentation.   **2**

    (c) Digital video and animation will often feature in multimedia presentations.

    Describe in detail how an animation is produced.   **2**

    (d) Compression techniques are used on video clips before they are stored and incorporated into multimedia presentations.

       (i) Explain why compression is needed.

       (ii) Apart from compression, how else can the storage requirements of a video clip be reduced?   **2**

    (e) When played back, a compressed video can be of lower quality than the original.

       (i) Explain why this happens.

       (ii) If compression is still to be used, how can this reduction in quality be prevented?   **2**

Marks

SECTION III

Part D—Multimedia Technology (continued)

Answer either Question 39 or Question 40

39. Creators and users of multimedia applications frequently buy upgrades to their sound and video cards.

    (*a*) Describe **two** developments in sound card technology that have contributed to the growth in multimedia products.   **2**

    (*b*) Describe **two** similarities in the way sound and video cards work.   **2**

    (*c*) When recording speech to be incorporated into a presentation, the presenter coughs. Explain how this could be edited out of the audio clip.   **2**

    (*d*) An audio file saved as CD quality will take a considerable amount of backing storage. Describe **two** ways, other than compression, in which the size of an audio file can be made smaller.   **2**

    (*e*) Many people who use their computers at home listen to internet audio, played through their computer, whilst they are working on another application.

    Describe **two** effects that this could have on system performance.   **2**

[Turn over

Marks

SECTION III

Part D—Multimedia Technology (continued)

40. Dr Michaelson has been asked to give a lecture at a medical conference. He is creating a multimedia presentation for use during his talk.

(a) As part of the presentation, he will be playing several sound files. He is considering which file formats to use for these.

 (i) What is meant by a sound file format?

 (ii) Name **one** sound file format and say in what particular circumstances it would be used. 2

(b) When gathering information for the lecture he scans images and text documents. He saves all documents as GIF files in error.

 (i) Describe GIF format.

 (ii) Name **one** other graphics format he could use and say why it would be better than GIF.

 (iii) OCR software could be used on the scanned text documents before they are included in the presentation. Give **two** advantages to Dr Michaelson of doing this. 4

(c) Describe in detail **one** method of video compression. 2

(d) The lecture will be videoed and saved as a compressed digital file. The video has to be edited before distribution.

 Describe **two** features of video editing software. 1

(e) The lecture video and presentation will be available to any member of the medical profession who wants a copy.

 Give **one** advantage of using DVD-R rather than a CD-RW as a storage medium for the two files. 1

[END OF SECTION III PART D]

[END OF QUESTION PAPER]

Dear Student

In 2005 the format of the Higher Computing exam was changed. Two exams were available, one following the format of previous years in this book. This format will not be available in 2006 and beyond.

The following Specimen Question Paper and the actual 2005 exam will give you good practice in the new format. However, the previous years' exams in this book will provide just as good revision and exam-practice features.

Here is some information about the new exam format:

The Question Paper
- contains 3 sections
- is worth up to 140 marks
- is allowed 2 hours 30 minutes.

Section I - 30 marks
- You are expected to attempt all questions in this section, writing short answers.
- The questions test your knowledge and understanding and problem-solving skills in the two mandatory units (Software Development and Computer Systems).
- Approximately 20 marks will be for knowledge and understanding.
- Approximately 10 marks will be for fairly straightforward problem-solving in familiar contexts.

Section II - 60 marks
- You are expected to attempt all questions in this section, writing longer answers that show your structuring and reasoning skills.
- The questions test your knowledge and understanding and problem-solving skills in the two mandatory units (Software Development and Computer Systems).
- Most questions will subdivided into a number of connected parts with the marks for each part clearly indicated.
- The questions test both knowledge and understanding and problem-solving in less familiar and more complex contexts than those in Section I.
- Approximately 20 marks will be for knowledge and understanding.
- Approximately 40 marks will be for problem-solving.

Section III - 50 marks
- This section has three sub-sections, one for each of the optional units (Artificial Intelligence, Computer Networking and Multimedia Technology).
- You are expected to tackle all the questions within one sub-section, writing longer answers that show your structuring and reasoning skills.
- Most questions will subdivided into a number of connected parts with the marks for each part clearly indicated.
- The questions test both knowledge and understanding and problem-solving in less familiar and more complex contexts than those in Section I.
- Approximately 17 marks will be for knowledge and understanding.
- Approximately 33 marks will be for problem solving.
- Some questions, or parts of questions, will need you to use knowledge from the mandatory units.

Please visit *www.sqa.org.uk* for further details.

[BLANK PAGE]

[C206/SQP238]

Computing

Higher

Specimen Question Paper

for use in and after 2005

Time 2 hours 30 minutes

NATIONAL
QUALIFICATIONS

Attempt **all** questions in Section I.

Attempt **all** questions in Section II.

Attempt **one** sub-section of Section III.

Part A	Artificial Intelligence	Page 10	Questions 18 to 22
Part B	Computer Networking	Page 14	Questions 23 to 26
Part C	Multimedia Technology	Page 16	Questions 27 to 30

For the sub-section chosen, attempt **all** questions.

Read all questions carefully.

Do not write on the question paper.

Write as neatly as possible.

SCOTTISH
QUALIFICATIONS
AUTHORITY

©

SECTION I

Attempt all questions in this section.

Marks

1. A processor has a 16 bit address bus. The processor is to write to memory location 800.

   (a) Describe the purpose of the address bus. **1**

   (b) Calculate the binary number that will be placed on the address bus. **2**

   (c) A register will hold the address of the location to be written to.

   Describe **one** other function of a register. **1**

2. A computer company has decided to use Unicode to replace ASCII.

   Describe **one** advantage of the use of Unicode over ASCII. **1**

3. Lauren buys a new digital camera. It stores its images on a flashcard and has a standard interface.

   (a) Describe **two** benefits of using a camera with a flashcard. **2**

   (b) The software distributed with the camera allows the photos to be saved in a number of different *standard file formats*. Name a "standard file format" suitable for this application and give **one** advantage and **one** disadvantage of its use. **3**

4. Declan notices that his computer's hard drive is running out of free space and that files take longer to load than they used to.

   (a) Name a utility program that could improve the speed at which files load. **1**

   (b) Describe how this software works. **1**

   (c) Explain how it improves loading time. **1**

5. What is a bootstrap loader? **2**

6. State **two** tasks carried out by the project manager during the development of software. **2**

7. (a) Describe what is meant by *top down design* and *stepwise refinement*. **2**

   (b) Describe **one** benefit of using top down design and stepwise refinement. **1**

8. Programs are required to be *robust* and *reliable*. Explain both of these terms. **2**

Marks

SECTION I (continued)

9. (*a*) The software development process can be described as *iterative*.

   What is meant by the term "iterative"? **1**

   (*b*) Give **one** example of iteration which may take place within the analysis stage. **1**

10. A program has been produced to store and process names and the times of competitors in a 100 metres sprint. A section of the data is shown below:

Name	Time (secs)
Ali Kidd	12.13
Roberta Young	13.67
Molly O'Neill	12.34

   (*a*) What data structure and data type could be used within the program to store the runners' times? **2**

   (*b*) The fastest runner has to be found. Which of the following algorithm would be used within the program in order to find the fastest runner?

   - Counting Occurences
   - Finding the maximum
   - Finding the minimum
   - Linear Search **1**

11. (*a*) Describe what is meant by a *scripting language*. **1**

   (*b*) Give **two** benefits of using a "scripting language". **2**

   (30)

[END OF SECTION I]

Marks

SECTION II

Attempt all questions in this section.

12. Helen is trying to buy a new computer. She will be creating and using several very large spreadsheet files with complex calculations. She has been reading the following two advertisements.

Lynx 983	**Ruath CM**
3·1 GHz AtheleteII Processor	2·9 GHz MDA4 Processor
512 Mb RAM	512 Mb RAM
120 Gb Hard Disk	32 Mb Cache
1·44 Mb Floppy Drive	100 Gb Hard Disk
DVD-ROM Drive (CD-ROM compatible)	DVD/CD-RW Combination Drive

(a) If the ability to back-up data is the most important factor for choosing a new computer, which computer would you suggest Helen buys? Give **two** reasons for your choice. 2

(b) Explain the effect of a *cache* on the performance of a computer. 2

Helen thinks that the Lynx 983 will be the faster computer because "it has a faster *clock speed*".

(c) (i) Describe **two** weaknesses of "clock speed" as a measure of processor performance.

(ii) Name and describe **one** other measure of processing power. 4

13. A school classroom has a local area network consisting of twenty computers and three servers. The teacher says that the network is a *client-server network*.

(a) The network could have been a *peer-to-peer network*.

(i) Describe **two** main differences between client-server and peer-to-peer networks.

(ii) Give **two** reasons why a client-server network is more suitable for a school classroom. 4

(b) One of the servers on the network is a *fileserver*. Name **one** other type of server that might be connected to the network and describe its purpose. 2

A computer which is connected to a network can be more liable to virus infections than others. Because of this an anti-virus utility has been installed on all network stations.

(c) Name and describe **one** class of virus that an anti-virus utility might detect. 2

Marks

SECTION II (continued)

13. (continued)

(*d*) Being connected to a network is one reason why one computer might be more liable to virus infection than others.

Give **two** other reasons why one computer might be more liable to virus infection than others.

2

14. Describe the stages of the *fetch execute cycle*.

Your answer should refer to appropriate buses and control lines.

5

15. A multimedia catalogue to help identify and record sightings of birds common to the UK is being constructed. The software will contain colour pictures and recordings of bird calls. It will allow users to browse through the existing information and to print off selected items.

(*a*) (i) Name a suitable class of application package to produce the catalogue.

(ii) Justify your answer in terms of the objects and operations involved. No credit will be given for naming proprietary software.

3

(*b*) The photographs of the birds will aid identification. Each photograph is 200 by 200 pixels and is stored in 32 bit colour. What is the file size of a single image?

Show all your working and give your answer in appropriate units.

4

(*c*) Part of the program will ask the user for the name of a bird and search a list of names to see if it exists. What data structure and data type will be used to hold the list?

2

(*d*) The part of program described in part (*c*) will display the **position** of the name in the list. For example, if the name is third in the list, the number 3 is displayed. If the name is not in the list a zero is displayed.

Use *pseudocode* to show how this section of program will search the list and display the appropriate value on screen.

6

Marks

SECTION II (continued)

16.   A game is being designed and the following pseudocode has been produced for part of the program.

Level 1 Algorithm

```
1    Initialise variables
2    Set up screen
3    Get user details
4    Start game loop
5      Get user move
6      Check for user win
7      Generate computer move
8      Check for computer win
9    End loop when win = true
10   Display message
11   End game
```

Refinement of Step 6

```
6.1 If number of counters in play = 0 then
6.2   Set win = true
6.3   Display player's name has won
6.4 End if statement
```

(a)   Some of the variables that will be initialised in line 1 of the algorithm are *global variables*. Explain **one** problem that the developers might have if they only use global variables in the program.

2

(b)   The three variables used by the "Check for user win" subroutine are **counters**, **win** and **name**. These variables can be either *called by reference* or *called by value*.

   (i)   Explain the meaning of the two terms *called by reference* and *called by value*.

   (ii)   For **each** of the three variables, state if the variable is "called by reference" or "called by value".

   Give a reason for **each** of your choices.

5

Marks

SECTION II (continued)

17. A new payroll system is being written by a software design company.

   (*a*) The first stage of the project provided the client with a formal specification document for the planned software. Give **two** reasons why the software company needs this document.

2

   (*b*) The software company has decided to make use of module libraries.

   Give **two** benefits to the software company of using module libraries.

2

   (*c*) During the production of the payroll system the software developers use both an *interpreter* and a *compiler*. Describe when each of these translator programs are used and give a reason for its use.

4

   (*d*) Part of the program will manipulate the details of each employee to produce an employee code. The code is produced by taking the first five letters of the surname then adding on their initial and the year they joined the company as follows:

   Set stem to first five characters of surname
   Set initial to first character of firstname
   Set employee code to stem + initial + year

   Firstname: **Gayle**
   Surname: **Dorward**
   Year Joined Company: **1999**

   (i) What is the employee code generated for Gayle Dorward?

   (ii) The name Joseph Li generates an error message. Using pseudocode like that above, rewrite the algorithm that creates the employee code to prevent this error from occurring.

3

   (*e*) After the payroll system has been in place for a few weeks the client asks the software company to carry out *adaptive* maintenance.

   (i) What is adaptive maintenance? Give an example to illustrate your answer.

   (ii) Who is most likely to meet the cost of the adaptive maintenance?

   Justify your answer.

4

(60)

[END OF SECTION II]

[BLANK PAGE]

Page eight

SECTION III

Attempt ONE sub-section of Section III

Part A   Artificial Intelligence   Page 10   Questions 18 to 22
Part B   Computer Networking   Page 14   Questions 23 to 26
Part C   Multimedia Technology   Page 16   Questions 27 to 30

For the sub-section chosen, attempt all questions.

Marks

SECTION III

Part A—Artificial Intelligence

Attempt all questions.

18. A computer that is capable of understanding natural language is intelligent.

    (a) Do you agree with this statement? Make **two** clear points to justify your answer. **2**

    (b) The Turing test was proposed as a test for artificial intelligence.

        (i) Describe the Turing test.

        (ii) Describe **two** limitations of the Turing test. **4**

    (c) Describe **two** difficulties of natural language processing giving examples to illustrate your answers. **4**

    (d) Practical applications of natural language processing include natural language database interfaces and natural language search engines. Describe **two** advantages of using natural language in these applications. **2**

    (e) Embedded technology is considered to be a growth area particularly in domestic appliances. The "smart" fridge may have a number of features including communication with its manufacturer.

        (i) Suggest **one** advantage for the customer of a fridge which has communication links to the manufacturer.

        (ii) Suggest **one** advantage for the manufacturer of this feature.

        (iii) Describe **one** other use for embedded technology in a fridge. **3**

19. An online car sales company decides to introduce an expert system to advise customers about the most suitable type of car for them.

    (a) Is this a suitable domain for the creation of such an expert system? Give **two** reasons for your answer. **2**

    (b) Consideration was given to creating the expert system using a procedural language or an expert system shell.

        (i) Explain **fully** the difference between an expert system and an expert system shell.

        (ii) Give **two** reasons to support implementation using a procedural language. **4**

    (c) The company insists that the expert system should be capable of *justification*. Describe **two** advantages of including this feature. **2**

Marks

SECTION III

Part A—Artificial Intelligence (continued)

20. (*a*) A mathematician draws the following diagram.

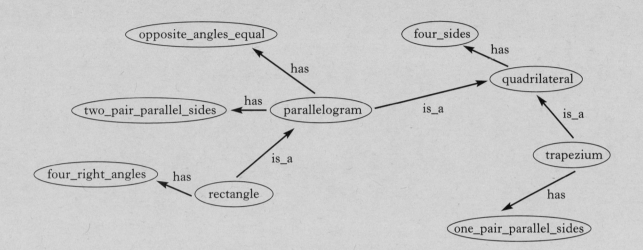

  (i) What is the name for the type of diagram drawn by the mathematician?

  (ii) Which stage of the software development process would result in such a diagram? Justify your answer.

  (iii) Describe **two** benefits of representing the knowledge in this way. **4**

(*b*) The mathematician decides to add the following information.

A rhombus is a kind of parallelogram. It has four equal sides.

Show how this information would be added to the diagram. You do not need to redraw the entire diagram. **2**

Marks

SECTION III

Part A—Artificial Intelligence (continued)

21. The following knowledge base was created using the information from the mathematician's diagram.

```
1   is_a (parallelogram, quadrilateral)
2   is_a (trapezium), quadrilateral)
3   is_a (rectangle, parallelogram)

4   has (quadrilateral, four_sides)
5   has (trapezium, one_pair_parallel_sides)
6   has (parallelogram, two_pair_parallel_sides)
7   has (parallelogram,opposite_angles_equal)
8   has (rectangle, four_right_angles)

9   has (X, Y) if
    is_a (X, Z) and
    has (Z, Y)
```

(a) Assuming a depth-first search is used to find the solution to the following query.

```
? has (rectangle, Y)
```

State the **four** solutions to the query in the order in which they would be found.   4

(b) Trace the steps in the search as far as the third solution.   5

(c) (i) What is the solution to the following query?

```
?-not (is_a (trapezium, quadrilateral)
```

(ii) Explain how this query would be evaluated.   2

(d) Rule 9 gives this knowledge base a feature known as *inheritance*.

   (i) What is inheritance?

   (ii) Give **one** advantage of inheritance.   2

Marks

SECTION III

Part A—Artificial Intelligence (continued)

22. Chess has been successfully implemented by Artificial Intelligence programmers. To decide which move to make the computer generates all the legal moves from certain position and chooses the one which gives the greatest advantage. In one particular implementation the program looks three moves ahead.

(*a*) When searching for the winning move a depth-first or breadth-first search could be used.

Give **one** advantage and **one** disadvantage of using a depth-first search rather than a breadth-first search.

2

(*b*) The choice of a good move can be made using a heuristic.

(i) Describe the use of a heuristic for selecting a move in chess.

(ii) Describe **two** advantages of using a heuristic over exhaustive search techniques.

4

(*c*) Define the term *combinatorial explosion* in relation to search techniques.

2

(50)

[END OF SECTION III—PART A]

Marks

SECTION III

Part B—Computer Networking

Attempt all questions.

23. Jamie has a Wireless Application Protocol (WAP) enabled communication device and is considering writing his own version of a currency converter program, in Wireless Markup Language (WML), for the device. He has already written web pages in HTML.

    (a) Describe **two** tags used in HTML. 2

    (b) Jamie is designing the screens for his currency converter. WML does not have a full range of text formatting features. Describe one similarity and one difference when changing the font size in WML compared with HTML. 2

    (c) Jamie asked one of his friends to test his currency converter program. His friend said that he had got confused by Jamie's use of the headline facility provided in WML. Why might his friend have been confused? 1

    (d) Jamie believes that the Regulation of Investigatory Powers Act 2000 is in direct contradiction to other laws which guarantee individuals the right to privacy.

        (i) Describe **one** implication of this Act.

        (ii) Explain **one** argument in favour of the Regulation of Investigatory Powers Act 2000 and **one** against it. 6

24. Network performance is important to both the network manager and network users. There are many factors which can affect the network performance.

    (a) Some local area networks operate a system called CSMA/CD.

        (i) What does CSMA/CD stand for?

        (ii) Describe fully how using CSMA/CD affects network performance. 5

    (b) (i) Describe fully how packet switching operates in a wide area network.

        (ii) Explain why packet switching may be used in preference to circuit switching. 5

    (c) Network performance is poor if there are errors in received data. Parity checking is a simple method of detecting errors.

        (i) Explain how **odd** parity checks work. Use an example to illustrate your answer.

        (ii) Describe one problem that might arise when using odd parity checking. Use an example to illustrate your answer. 5

    (d) A cyclic redundancy check (CRC) is another method for checking for transmission errors.

        (i) Explain how a cyclic redundancy check works.

        (ii) Explain the effect of cyclic redundancy checking on the *speed* and *accuracy* of a network. Justify your answer. 5

Page fourteen

Marks

SECTION III

Part B—Computer Networking (continued)

25. An increasing number of companies are now subject to the "Denial of Service attack".

    (a) Explain what happens when a company is the subject of a Denial of Service attack. **3**

    (b) Describe **three** features of a firewall that might prevent a Denial of Service attack. **3**

26. The Open System Interconnection (OSI) model breaks the operation of a computer network into seven layers.

    (a) Which layer provides basic error detection and correction to ensure that data sent is the same as data received? **1**

    (b) The Presentation Layer can apply compression techniques to data before it is sent over the network. Which layer decompresses the data? **1**

    (c) Describe the structure of a Class A IP address. **2**

    (d) A school has a local area network with one hundred computers connected to it.

        (i) Why is Class A IP addressing **not** suitable for this network?

        (ii) Which Class of IP address would you suggest that the school uses? Justify your answer. **3**

    (e) E-commerce uses OSI network protocols. A small Highland company has recently won an award for its Internet-based mail order business. Their web site offers a multimedia guide to their products and they can receive orders via the web site. Creating the web site was a considerable financial investment for the company.

        (i) Give **two** benefits to the company of having the web site.

        (ii) Some potential customers of the company might be cautious of buying the goods across the Internet. Explain why this might be so.

        (iii) Suggest **two** actions that the company could have taken to reassure their customers. **6**

    (50)

[END OF SECTION III—PART B]

Marks

SECTION III

Part C—Multimedia Technology

Attempt all questions.

27. When creating web pages many different elements of multimedia can be used. One example is 2D graphics.

    (a) Name **one** item of hardware that can be used to capture a 2D graphic and **explain clearly** how it converts the graphic into digital data.   3

    (b) Some graphics are stored as JPEGs. However it has been decided that these graphics must be used for animation purposes and so they are converted to GIFs.

      (i) Explain why *dithering* is used in this situation.

      (ii) Describe how dithering works in this case.   3

    (c) The GIF file could be stored as *interlaced* or *non-interlaced*.

      (i) Explain how each of these two types of GIFs are displayed.

      (ii) Explain **one** advantage of using interlaced compared with non-interlaced graphics for web pages.   4

    (d) A GIF image of 640×480 resolution needs to be stored. Calculate its file size.   3

28. Picture A shows an image of a cylinder. This image has been changed to look like Picture B.

    Picture A   Picture B

    (a) Describe **two** features of 3D software which have been used to change Picture A into Picture B.   2

    (b) Virtual Reality Mark Up Language (VRML) could be used to create Picture B (above). An example of the code is given below:

    ```
    Cylinder {
    radius 1·0
    height 2·0
    }
    ```

      (i) Write down the VRML for a sphere.

      (ii) Give **two** benefits of using VRML when creating 3D images.

      (iii) Explain the need for the VRML header when using a browser.   4

Marks

SECTION III

Part C—Multimedia Technology (continued)

28. (continued)

The use of multimedia technologies and its applications has increased dramatically over the past decade.

(c) Explain how the following have increased multimedia capabilities.

(i) CODEC hardware/software

(ii) Data communications   **4**

(d) Describe the term "streaming" when used within multimedia.   **1**

29. When recording video for multimedia presentations, the method used for storing the video frames is important to reduce the file size and aid compatibility.

(a) Describe how video is stored using:

(i) MPEG

(ii) AVI.   **4**

(b) Apart from compression, describe **two** methods which could be used to reduce the size of a video data file.   **2**

(c) Calculate the file size of a 4 second video clip captured at a resolution of 800×600 at a frame rate of 25 frames per second with a 24 bit colour depth. Show all working and express your answer in appropriate units.   **3**

(d) The way video is recorded works like this:

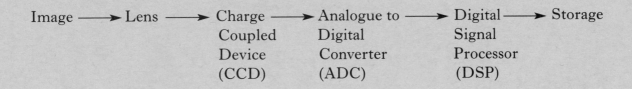

(i) Explain the role of the CCD.

(ii) Explain the role of the DSP.

(iii) Explain the benefit of using a digital camera which has three CCDs instead of a single CCD.   **6**

(e) Describe **two** types of **transition** that can be used to link video clips.   **2**

Marks

SECTION III

Part C—Multimedia Technology (continued)

30. A sound recording studio uses various techniques to record and store sound.

    (a) State **two** different functions a sound card could perform when capturing sound.   2

    (b) Describe how RAW data files are stored.   2

    (c) Name and describe **one** file format other than RAW for storing sound.   2

    (d) Calculate the amount of storage required to store a 2 minute stereo sample at 16 bit resolution sampled at 44·1 kHz.   3

                                                                                (50)

[END OF SECTION III—PART C]

[END OF QUESTION PAPER]

Page eighteen

[BLANK PAGE]

X206/301

NATIONAL
QUALIFICATIONS
2005

MONDAY, 30 MAY
1.00 PM – 3.30 PM

COMPUTING
HIGHER

Attempt **all** questions in Section I.

Attempt **all** questions in Section II.

Attempt **one** sub-section of Section III.

Part A	Artificial Intelligence	Page 10	Questions 24 to 28
Part B	Computer Networking	Page 13	Questions 29 to 32
Part C	Multimedia Technology	Page 16	Questions 33 to 36

For the sub-section chosen, attempt **all** questions.

Read all questions carefully.

Do not write on the question paper.

Write as neatly as possible.

SCOTTISH
QUALIFICATIONS
AUTHORITY

©

SECTION I

Attempt all questions in this section.

Marks

1. (a) What is a *buffer*? **1**

   (b) Explain the function of a buffer within a *printer interface*. **2**

2. In *floating point notation* what defines:

   (i) the range; **1**

   (ii) the precision or accuracy; **1**

   of the numbers stored?

3. Describe how graphics are stored using a *bit-mapped* package. **2**

4. Describe the function of a *defragmenter*. **3**

5. A network has a file server and a print server.

   Name **one** other type of server that the network may have. **1**

6. (a) What is the number **385** represented as a binary number? **1**

   (b) Represent the number **–86** in **8-bit** *Two's Complement*. **1**

7. Lambside Council want to network their stand-alone computers.

   What piece of hardware will need to be present in their computers to allow this to happen? **1**

8. Magnus has created a graphic file at home. The computers at school use a different graphics application.

   Name a standard file format that the file could be saved in to allow **both** applications to read the same file. **1**

9. Give **one** reason why increasing the amount of cache memory can improve system performance. **1**

10. A *software specification* is produced at the analysis stage of the software development cycle.

    State the purpose of this document. **1**

Marks

SECTION I (continued)

11. Describe **two** techniques used by the systems analyst for extracting information at the analysis stage of the software development cycle.   2

12. An employee with a disability makes use of a specialised input device. However it does not work with a recently installed piece of software.

    What type of maintenance would be required to alter the software to accept this type of input device? Justify your answer.   2

13. *Pseudocode* is a design notation used to design a solution to a problem.

    (a) Describe what is meant by "pseudocode".   1

    (b) Name and describe **one** other design notation which could be used.   2

14. What type of variable can be accessed from anywhere in a program?   1

15. A program has been created to process a list of 50 names.

    Identify the data structure and data type that could be used to store this list of names within the program.   2

16. A group of students are working together to create a piece of software for a local playgroup. The lecturer tells them that *module libraries* can be used.

    Identify **two** benefits of using module libraries when constructing code.   2

17. The software in Question 16 is to be written in a procedural language.
    Give **one** reason why a procedural language has been chosen for this task.   1

    (30)

[END OF SECTION I]

[Turn over

Marks

SECTION II

Attempt all questions in this section.

18. Peter runs a photography store. He develops and prints photographs in various formats.

    (a) He decides to offer a "red-eye" removal service on all digital images.

    Would he use bit-mapped graphic or vector graphic software? Explain your answer.   2

    (b) An image is 4 × 6 inches, has a resolution of 800 dpi and each pixel can display 65536 different colours.

    Calculate the storage requirements for this image.

    Express your answer using suitable units. Show **all** working.   4

    (c) Customers bring their image files into the shop on flash cards and CD-R.

    Peter has to be able to read the files from these different formats.

    Explain **one** advantage of each format over the other for the customer.   2

    (d) Peter is replacing his colour inkjet printer.

    Describe **one** technical characteristic that the printer should have.

    Justify your answer.   2

19. Joe is playing a game program on his computer. The processor in Joe's computer uses a 24-bit *data bus* and a 32-bit *address bus*. The computer has a USB *interface*.

    (a) Calculate the maximum amount of memory which Joe's computer could address. Express your answer using suitable units.   3

    (b) Two functions of an interface are *data format conversion* and handling of *status signals*. Describe both of these functions.   2

    (c) Joe read that clock speed and data bus width are both indicators of processor performance.

        (i) Name **two** other methods of **measuring** processor performance.   2

        (ii) Describe each of the methods named in part (i).   2

    (d) A new highest score is to be written to the high score table in the game. This is done by a *memory write* operation. Describe how a typical processor would carry out a "memory write" operation. Your answer should mention the buses used at each stage.   4

Marks

SECTION II (continued)

20. (a) Connaidh buys a new web design creation package. She finds that it will not run on her computer. Suggest **two** reasons for this.   2

(b) This image was created in a *vector graphics* package.

State **two** operations that could be carried out on the object.   2

(c) Memory management will perform a number of tasks during the loading of a file.

Describe **one** of these tasks.   1

(d) When using the software, Connaidh is worried about breaching the Copyright, Designs and Patents Act. Describe **two** ways in which she could breach copyright.   2

(e) State **two** techniques that anti-virus software may use in the **detection** of a virus.   2

21. A website has been created by a software house for a bank. A program has been written to count and record the number of times each page linked to the home page is visited or "hit".

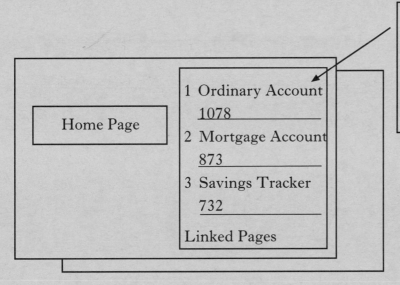

Linked web page indicating number of "hits"

Linked page 1 has been visited **1078** *times*

(a) The evaluation stage is part of the Software Development Process.

How does this evaluation benefit:

(i) the bank;   1

(ii) the project manager of the software house?   1

(b) One of the software house's aims is to ensure a *reliable* program.

(i) Explain what the term "reliable" means.   1

(ii) Describe fully **one** method the software house could use to ensure that the program is reliable **before** the software is released.   1

[Turn over

Marks

SECTION II (continued)

21. (continued)

(c) The number of hits for each page is stored in an array called Hits().

Using the example in the diagram above

$$Hits(1) = 1078$$

Using a design notation with which you are familiar, write an **algorithm** which would find the number of the page with the maximum number of hits within the website. **6**

(d) Bank employees also need to search and use other websites.

One problem they experience is that web pages take a long time to download.

Describe a possible reason for this problem. **1**

22. A computer program to run the registration process at Dunwearie High School is being developed.

(a) It is very important that the finished software is *robust*. Explain what the term "robust" means. **1**

(b) The software uses parameters throughout. These are either call *by reference* or call *by value*.

(i) Describe what is meant by the term call "by reference".

Your answer should refer to the mechanism by which this is achieved. **2**

(ii) Describe what is meant by the term call "by value".

Your answer should refer to the mechanism by which this is achieved. **2**

(iii) Give **one** advantage of using call "by value" compared with call "by reference".

Justify your answer. **2**

Marks

SECTION II (continued)

23. A mail order company requires a piece of software to be developed that will store and process customer details. The software house are considering creating a specialised program or using an application package which supports scripting.

(a) Describe **two** uses for scripting languages.　　2

(b) The software house decide to use a high level language to create the package.

Event-driven and *declarative languages* could be used.

(i) Describe what "event-driven" and "declarative" languages are.　　2

(ii) For each of the languages given in (i), give **one** reason why that type of language may be suitable for the mail order company's purpose.　　2

(c) The programmers use both a *compiler* and *interpreter* when constructing the code.

(i) Why would an interpreter be used when developing the software?　　2

(ii) Explain in terms of *efficiency* the difference between using a compiler compared with an interpreter when translating code related to the pseudocode below.

```
1  loop 300 times
2     ask user for name
3     store name in array
4  end loop
```

Your answer should include both processor time and memory usage for each type of translator.　　2

(60)

[END OF SECTION II]

[Turn over

[BLANK PAGE]

SECTION III

Attempt ONE sub-section of Section III

Part A	Artificial Intelligence	Page 10	Questions 24 to 28
Part B	Computer Networking	Page 13	Questions 29 to 32
Part C	Multimedia Technology	Page 16	Questions 33 to 36

For the sub-section chosen, attempt *all* questions.

Marks

SECTION III

Part A—Artificial Intelligence

Attempt all questions.

24. A knowledge base has been created to describe some of our solar system.

   1 star(the_sun).   (The sun is a star.)

   2 planet(the_earth).   (The earth is a planet.)

   3 planet(saturn).

   4 planet(neptune).

   5 orbits(the_earth, the_sun).   (The earth orbits the sun.)

   6 orbits(mars, the_sun).

   7 orbits(saturn, the_sun).

   8 orbits(titan, saturn).

   9 orbits(nereid, neptune).

   10 satellite(X Y)if orbits(X, Y).   (X is a satellite of Y if
                                                   X orbits Y.)

   11 satellite(X Y) if orbits(X, Z)and   (X is a satellite of Y if X
                         satellite(Z, Y).   orbits Z and Z is a satellite
                                                   of Y.)

   (a) What would be the first solution for each of the following queries?

      (i) ? orbits(nereid, X).

      (ii) ? planet(X) and orbits(Y, X).

   (b) Assuming a depth-first search is used, explain how the program would   1
       find solutions to the following query. You should use the line numbers to
       exemplify your answer.   2

       ? satellite(titan, Y).

                                                                                 6

Marks

SECTION III

Part A—Artificial Intelligence (continued)

24. (continued)

(c) A moon is to be defined as an object that orbits a planet.

Design a "moon_of" rule for use in the knowledge base.   **3**

(d) Describe a problem that would be encountered when trying to extend the knowledge base to describe all known stars. Explain your answer.   **2**

25. Valuable objects are found by people using metal detectors and by other activities such as digging the garden. Such objects are the subject of common law in Scotland and a company has decided to provide legal advice using an expert system.

(a) An expert system has an *inference engine*. Describe the function of this component.   **1**

(b) The fully tested expert system is made available on the World Wide Web and a user follows the advice given. However, the advice is wrong because the law is different in their country.

   (i) Explain whether the user can be held responsible for breaking the law.   **2**

   (ii) Describe **two** other limitations of an expert system when providing legal advice.   **2**

(c) The expert system was not created using a procedural language.

Give **one** reason why a procedural language was not used.   **1**

(d) Describe **one** advantage of using expert systems for legal advice.   **1**

26. A hospital holds many text-based reports of patient interviews in a computerised database. They decide to introduce *natural language processing* to help with the searching of the system. The system **does not** use speech input or speech recognition of any kind.

(a) (i) Describe what is meant by "natural language processing".   **2**

   (ii) Describe **two** problems associated with "natural language processing" using an example to illustrate your answer.   **4**

(b) A doctor wants to search for cases where "pneumonia" has been found.

A search in the old database would result in matches such as:

"pneumonia cannot be excluded"
"rule out pneumonia"
"pneumonia was confirmed"

Using the examples above explain why a search system using "natural language processing" would be more efficient, by excluding irrelevant matches.   **2**

Marks

SECTION III

Part A—Artificial Intelligence (continued)

26. (continued)

(c) State **two** advances in hardware and explain how **each** has aided the development of natural language processing.

4

27. A new car has a navigation system with 5000 destinations. It is able to find a route between the driver's start point and destination.

(a) For the search tree shown below write down the order the nodes would be visited using:

(i) breadth-first;

1

(ii) depth-first.

1

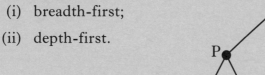

(b) The navigation system has a small amount of memory.

Explain which search method should be used.

2

(c) Explain how *parallel processing* could speed up route finding.

3

(d) The *Turing test* is a test for machine intelligence. Describe how the test could be used to determine if the navigation system has intelligence.

3

28. A building society lends money to people so that they can buy a house.

A house valuation depends on factors such as:

• location of the house given by postcode
• number of rooms

The building society has access to all this information and accurate valuations of a large number of houses. The building society decides to use this data to create an *artificial neural system* (neural network) to value houses.

(a) Give **two** reasons why this problem is suitable for the creation of a *neural network* (artificial neural system).

2

(b) A strength of a "neural network" is its ability to learn.

(i) Describe the structure of a "neural network".

3

(ii) Describe how the neural network for valuing houses would be trained.

2

(50)

[END OF SECTION III—PART A]

Marks

SECTION III

Part B—Computer Networking

Attempt all questions.

29. International Pencils is a multinational office supplies manufacturer with branch offices in seven European capital cities. These branch offices are connected in a wide-area network (WAN) to allow financial data to flow around the company.

   (a) When setting up the WAN, the company used *dedicated leased lines*.

   State **one** advantage and **one** disadvantage of leased-lines when compared to using the public telephone broadband network.　　2

   (b) The company network conforms to the Open Systems Interconnection (OSI) model.

   Two layers of the OSI model are the *Data Link* layer and *Network* layer.

   (i) Describe these two layers of the OSI model.　　4

   (ii) Name a networking device that operates at **each** of these levels.　　2

   (c) Explain why is it important that networks are designed using standard models, such as OSI.　　1

   (d) Each device on the International Pencils European network has a **24-bit** *MAC* code.

   (i) What does MAC stand for?　　1

   (ii) Explain why it is necessary for a device on the network to have a MAC code.　　1

   (iii) What is the **maximum** number of devices on this network?　　1

30. A group of students are planning to connect their computers together so that they can play *NetSpider*, a new multi-player network game. Updates for the game are available from the game developer's website.

   (a) The students could choose to use physical cables or a wireless LAN for their network.

   (i) Explain how a wireless LAN would operate.　　2

   (ii) Give **two** reasons why the students might choose a wireless LAN over cabling.　　2

   (b) The game updates are available at the IP address **127.47.86.23** or by going to the designer's web address at www.WebGrafters.co.uk

   (i) Briefly explain the **purpose** of an IP address.　　1

   (ii) How are the IP address and the web address related?　　2

[Turn over

Marks

SECTION III

Part B—Computer Networking (continued)

30. (continued)

(c) The updater file is transferred using a browser operating the *TCP/IP* standard internet protocol.

   (i) Describe how the transfer takes place under **TCP/IP**.   4

   (ii) Name **another** standard protocol that might be used to transfer this file.   1

(d) The connection used by the students to download the file is rated at **15 Megabits per second** (Mbps).

   (i) If the size of the updater file is 112 Megabytes, how long will it take to download at 15 Mbps?   2

   (ii) Give **two** reasons why it might take longer to download the file in practice.   2

31. Fragrant Futures is a charity dedicated to preserving wildflowers and older varieties of herbs and fruits. It plans to build an education centre with over 100 networked computers. This will allow school parties to access a very large central database of plants and run other educational software about nature conservation.

(a) Describe **two** different technological advances that have made the creation of such a network possible. Justify your answer.   4

(b) The database can be updated by registered users and is held on one computer.

   (i) Explain why it is necessary for this network to have a backup strategy.   1

   (ii) Describe a suitable backup strategy for use in this situation. You should make reference to hardware and software needed.   3

(c) Fragrant Futures has been the victim of a *denial of service* attack.

   Describe how a "denial of service" attack operates.   2

The charity has set up a website for students to access from outwith the education centre. The website has been created using HTML. The HTML code for one of the pages looks like this:

```
<html>
      <head>
      <title>   FRAGRANT FUTURES   </title>
      </head>
</html>
```

(d) Describe **two** other HTML tags that could be used for this page.   2

Marks

SECTION III

Part B—Computer Networking (continued)

31. (continued)

(*e*) The website includes a search facility that enables users to search the web for information about particular flowers. Describe **two** methods that could be used by this search facility to find the relevant information across the WWW.

2

(*f*) The charity wishes to sell some of their products on-line using this website.

  (i) Describe **two** benefits to the company of selling goods on-line.

2

  (ii) Describe **one** possible problem that could arise from selling goods on-line.

1

  (iii) Describe **two** possible solutions to your answer to Part (ii).

2

32. Data transmission on the network will either operate by *circuit-switching* or *packet-switching*.

(*a*) Explain the term "circuit-switching".

2

(*b*) Describe **one** advantage of **circuit-switching** over **packet-switching** for this network.

1

(50)

[END OF SECTION III—PART B]

[Turn over

Marks

SECTION III

Part C—Multimedia Technology

Attempt all questions.

33. Jamie wants to be able to put family photographs and movie clips into a multimedia presentation.

    He has between 400 and 500 old photographs and about 10 minutes of movie clips.

    (a) (i) Name a design notation or technique which would be suitable for **planning** this presentation.　1

    (ii) Give **two** reasons why your choice of notation or technique would be suitable for Jamie's task.　2

    (b) Jamie asks his relatives to provide audio comments for the photographs. Explain the steps he would follow to include the comments into his presentation. For each step you should include the relevant hardware and software. Your answer should include an appropriate level of technical detail.　5

    (c) Jamie makes a 20 second audio recording about one of the photos.

    It is sampled at 11kHz with 8-bit resolution in stereo.

    What is the uncompressed filesize of the recording? Express your answer in appropriate units.　4

    (d) Describe **two** techniques a multimedia creator may use to fully test the finished multimedia presentation.　2

34. Creators and users of multimedia applications frequently buy upgrades to their sound and video cards.

    (a) (i) Describe **two** developments in sound card technologies.　2

    (ii) Show how they have contributed to the growth in multimedia products.　2

    (b) *Digital Signal Processing* (DSP) is a feature of interface cards. What role does **Digital Signal Processing** play in these cards?　2

    (c) Describe **two** similarities, other than DSP, in the way sound and video cards work.　2

    (d) Holographic technology for storage of data will be welcomed by creators of large multimedia applications. State **one** improvement that holographic technology has made to the storage of data. Explain how this is achieved.　2

Marks

SECTION III

Part C—Multimedia Technology (continued)

35. Dr Michaelson is creating a multimedia presentation for use during a lecture.

(*a*) As part of the presentation, he will be playing several sound files. He is considering which file formats to use. Why would standard file formats be useful in this case?

2

(*b*) Dr Michaelson asks his assistant to send him some files in *Resource Interchange File Format* (RIFF). His assistant e-mails him with the following message:

"Have attached two files as you requested"

Dr Michaelson gets a little confused when he sees that the attachments are in WAV waveform file.

Explain in detail why the assistant had not made a mistake.

3

(*c*) Name **one** sound file format, other than WAV and RIFF (ADPCM), and recommend a particular purpose for which it would be used.

2

(*d*) Dr Michaelson is also going to use VRML files.

(i) What does VRML stand for?

1

(ii) What is VRML used for?

1

(iii) Why are VRML files an efficient way of downloading an image from the Internet?

3

[Turn over for Question 36 on *Page eighteen*

Marks

SECTION III

Part C—Multimedia Technology (continued)

36. The image below is the first frame of a thirty-second movie clip. The movie clip is in 24-bit colour.

(a) By referring to this frame, explain how the MPEG compression algorithm would be applied to this movie clip. 3

(b) The movie is compressed, but when played back it is of lower quality than the original.

   (i) State **two** reasons why this might have happened. 2

   (ii) For each of these reasons, state why the quality has been reduced. 2

(c) Compression is still to be used on the original movie.

   (i) State **two** ways that reduction in quality could be prevented. 2

   (ii) Explain how the quality is maintained by **each** of these. 2

(d) The cameraman who took the video now uses a Bluetooth-enabled digital video camera and a Bluetooth-enabled laptop computer instead of USB.

   (i) State **one** disadvantage of Bluetooth technology. 1

   (ii) Give **two** reasons why he finds his move to Bluetooth technology useful when downloading his video files at sports events. 2

(50)

[END OF SECTION III—PART C]

[END OF QUESTION PAPER]

Pocket answer section for
SQA Higher Computing
2001–2004, 2005 (Old Arrangements), 2005 SQP, 2005

© 2005 Scottish Qualifications Authority, All Rights Reserved
Published by Leckie & Leckie Ltd, 8 Whitehill Terrace, St Andrews, Scotland, KY16 8RN
tel: 01334 475656, fax: 01334 477392, enquiries@leckieandleckie.co.uk, www.leckieandleckie.co.uk

Computing Higher
2001

Section I

1. (a) Bus **or** Ring **or** Star (**NOT** *Mesh*)
    (*Have to accept tree—"star of stars"*)
    + Appropriate diagram with at least **one** relevant label
    Amendment—no half marks

    (b) Network card **or** NIC **or** networking card **or** Ethernet card (etc)

2. (a) When the processor is servicing a peripheral a buffer temporarily stores the data being sent in RAM (thus freeing the processor to carry out other tasks)

    (b) When printer is accessed over a network **or** When large files have to be dealt with **or** When advanced management of printing jobs has to be exercised (ordering, costing etc)

3. **Description based on:**
    editing (moving, resizing etc) eg can you select a part of the graphic by clicking on it; if so, vector
    Amount of storage required
    Resolution dependancy eg if it becomes "blocky", when enlarged then bit-mapped
    Quality of print outs

4. (a)
    $3 \times 4 \times 600 \times 600 \times 8 = 34\,560\,000$ bits
    $34\,560\,000/(8 \times 1024 \times 1024) = 4{\cdot}12$ Mb **or**
    $3 \times 4 \times 600 \times 600$ pixels $= 4\,320\,000$ pixels
    256 colours $\Rightarrow$ 1 byte per pixel $\Rightarrow 4\,320\,000$ bytes
    so $4\,320\,000/1024/1024$ Mb $= 4{\cdot}1$ Mb

    (b) Zip drive **or** Jazz drive **or** Hard Disc drive **or** DAT drive **or** CD-R drive (*not CD-ROM*) **or** DVD-R drive
    All of the above have enough storage capacity to store the file ie has more than $4{\cdot}1$ Mb capacity

5. (a) −128 to 127—*no alternative values, but allow* -2^7 *etc*

    (b) (i) Mantissa—precision is increased (*allow accuracy*)

    (ii) Exponent—range of numbers is increased

6. Components with two stable states are used to represent 0's and 1's

7. Each memory location is identified by a unique address.

8. (a) Counting Occurrences **or** (iii) **or** 3

    (b) User Guide
    Technical Guide

    (c) If changes have to be made to the guides then it is simpler to send out a new CD
    Also cheaper than printing out hard copies of new guides

9. (a) Analysis—understanding of client's problem into a precise specification, clarifying the requirements
    Design—planning of solution to problem, outlining the solution

    (b) The action of going back through a stage and rethinking, redoing
    A stage is revisited following testing or other further stage of refinement

10. (a) To allow other programmers to understand the code; In case changes have to be made later

    (b) Any **two** of the following:
    Modular code
    Internal commentary
    Indentation (accept structured listing)
    Meaningful variable and subprogram names/ identifiers

11. (i) editor—to enable creation of program source code, enter and make changes to code

    (ii) translator—to allow the program to run, convert HLL code into machine code

    (iii) error tracing tool—to enable the searching for logic errors throughout the code during controlled execution to help identify the location of errors
    Must make clear that error tracing is not about syntax errors

12. (a) (i) Local variable—variable used exclusively within subprogram, scope limited to a single subprogram

    (ii) Subprograms can be run separately from rest of code, if use local variables subprogram can only affect the value of a variable within the subprogram—all data transfer between subprograms must be made explicit using parameter passing

    (b) array
    data structure eg linked list etc

Computing Higher
2001 (cont.)

Section II

13. (a) (i) Status information: Device selection
Speed Conversion—to compensate for differences between processor and peripheral in terms of speed (ie buffering, latching);
Data representation—to convert analogue to digital, serial to parallel (accept voltage)

    (ii) To allow the connection of any peripheral to the computer
Many different peripherals on the market, too complex if each one had a different interface
So that no incompatibility problems arise between the peripheral and computer. To allow peripherals by different manufacturers to be compatible with most cpus

    (iii) Driver, hardware driver

(b) Difficult to compare different manufacturers as:
The actual process being carried out by a single instruction may be very different
Don't know how many instructions per second can be processed
The "speed" of the computer may depend on other factors such as internal bus widths, type of processor,
Speed of peripherals/interfaces USB etc
Use of cache (Level 2, Level 1)
Speed of memory bus (PC100, PC133 etc)
Different length of time to execute instruction

(c) Address bus must be 24 bits
Each location is 4 bytes long. $64/4 = 16$ so need $16 \times 1024 \times 1024$ locations (ie addresses)
ie $2^4 \times 2^{10} \times 2^{10} = 2^{24}$ addresses
No of addresses = $2^{\text{address bus width}}$
So address bus width is 24 bits

(d) Register with Data Protection Registrar
Keep data safe and secure
Update data regularly
Allow inspection of data by data subject
Correct errors in data if demonstrated
Adhere to registered disclosure protocol

14. (a) 1 User has to type from keyboard (not particularly easy for some), validity errors very likely
Endless possible entries could be given which the program would have to check
    2 Set number of entries chosen from menu, validity errors impossible
Good control of mouse required to select country, difficult for user to see all at once

14. (a) 3 Quickest method for user as typing in one character will restrict choices on screen
Set number of entries chosen from menu, validity errors possible but unlikely
Keyboard and/or mouse could be used

(b) Who will the typical users be?
level of knowledge of users? (will they be able to spell correctly?)
Is it comprehensive enough for end user?
Is speed of data entry an issue?

(c) Use range of test cases with suitable users
Experiment with typical end user ie have the program tested by **many** potential users;
test with a range of user **types**

(d) • Array of names stored for validation would need changed for all 3
• Menu choices changed for 2 and 3.
1 requires no change
• 2 requires editing of the list (probably a data file)
• 3 may also require some coding, although the algorithm for scrolling the list automatically should be generic, suitable for any country's name

15. (a) Video card—to input video frames
Large RAM—to view video on screen
Large backing storage—to allow editing of large video data files
High resolution, colour, high refresh rate monitor—for detailed editing work

(b) (i) Digital or optical zoom, LCD screen, resolution, colour depth, capacity
Accept also lens, media card requirements, bundled software

    (ii) No need to develop film or to buy film—so reduced time
No wastage of film if wrong shot taken, able to delete unwanted photos; data can be downloaded directly to computer for editing and storage; immediate hard copy possible

(c) • high resolution (over 600dpi) to give non-grainy images;
• must be colour rather than black/white
• "photo quality" ie larger number of inks, variable dot size etc

(d) database software (or searchable web pages) to store images
in structured way with keywords etc for searching
graphics storage requirements are likely to be high
so this would probably need to be held on a CD, so a CD-writer would be required
Alternatively
hierarchical folder structure with descriptive folder and file names
AND thumbnails of photographs as icons, etc

16. (a) *Two points along the lines of*:
The ability to attach code to an event such as a mouse click or a window opening.
Allows ease of interface design incorporating text, data entry boxes, buttons . . . ;
The availability of pre-written code to generate dialog boxes, buttons etc
non-linear program structure allows program to respond to events dictated by the user

(b) *Two points along the lines of*:
Programs written in procedural language have definite start/end points.
Order of execution determined by algorithm rather than events.
Fixed algorithm for execution of program, rather than depending on user.

(c) *Two brief descriptions of relevant functions such as*:
In file management system—loading or saving of data file
In input/Output system—mouse clicks, keystrokes buffered until application needs them
In memory management—allocate memory for data

(d) *Two points made from each of Advantages and Difficulties, such as:*
Advantages—no need for specialist programming knowledge as macros may be used to "program" applications; speed of development, as much of the functionality is already present within the application; data structures already exist; algorithms for searches and comparisons already exist

Difficulties—may be a lack of necessary functions within application eg storage and updating of totals might require global variables; Lack of flexibility in design of screen display—may be restricted by application may required coding in a scripting language (eg VBA); means user must have the appropriate application package

17. (a) IF mark >=0 AND mark <=100

(b) *Two points from*:
makes program more modular;
allows same variable names (eg loop counters) in more than one subprogram;
makes data flow explicit improving readability and therefore maintainability;
accept description of portability

(c) (i) no significant difference
(ii) 1-D array better, as makes clear the fact that the 10 marks are all related
(iii) much simpler to pass a single array than ten separate variables

(d) By Reference passes pointer rather than whole data structure
By Reference allows parameter to be altered in the procedure, whereas by value any changes within procedure are not passed out of the procedure

18. (a) List could be passed by value but most languages require arrays to be passed by reference.
Could also have a parameter called "found" type boolean (or integer) passed by value

(b) (position < size of list) AND (item not found) AND (still items in list to search)

(c) *Any two of*
smaller source code size
improved reliability since code already tested
reduced requirement for maintenance
debugging is simplified

(d) (i) removal of the condition "item not found"
(ii) require an array of data type integer to store list of positions
require a count of type integer to store number of items found

Section III
Part A—Artificial Intelligence

19. (a) (i) analysis and design
(ii) knowledge engineer extracts specialist knowledge from domain expert during analysis;
the design stage is done by the knowledge engineer with no input needed from domain expert

(b) (i) expert system = user interface + inference engine + knowledge base
expert system shell = user interface + inference engine (but no knowledge base)
(ii) no need to code user interface and inference engine; but may be less flexible

(c) (i) ADVISE wind speed increase (0·9) IF direction = S AND pressure falling
ADVISE wind speed increase (0·5) IF direction = N AND pressure falling
(ii) certainty factor (eg 0·9 for very likely, 0·5 for may) indicate the level of confidence in the advice
for certainty factor on its own
(iii) response should describe issue of legal accountability for information used

20. (a) (i) `X = scotland, Y = 4406`
(ii) `?mountain(X,scotland,_)`
`[could have a variable`
`instead of_]`

(b) match clause 6; instantiate X to ben-nevis;
first sub-goal
`mountain(ben_nevis,scotland,H);`
match at clause 3; instantiate H=4406;
2nd sub-goal 4406>3000 is TRUE, so
`munro(ben_nevis)` is TRUE

(c) `furth(X) if mountain(X,Y,Z) and`
`Z>3000 and not Y=scotland`

Computing Higher
2001 (cont.)

20. (d) (i) `munro(X) if height(X,H) and country(X,scotland) and H>3000`

      (ii) search time will be longer
due to the greater number of clauses

21. (a) finding a representation for the current state of the game (positions of pieces); there are many rules to be coded; the number of positions multiplies very quickly and unmanageably when looking ahead; the need for a function which can evaluate possible positions

    (b) need not just the development but also the impact
hugely increased processor speeds allow large numbers of positions to be evaluated in a reasonably short time
huge increases in memory allow many possible game positions to be stored simultaneously
parallel processing allows subdivision of the search task

    (c) heuristics allow a smaller number of probably better moves to be selected from the large number of possible moves, thus speeding up the process of determining the next move

    (d) ability to learn from successes and failures, so that performance improved over time

    (e) (i) any description related to machine learning, creativity, natural language processing, pattern recognition (context) "justified" reasoning. Vision systems

        (ii) either an area of human ability must be described with a reason why technology could never out-perform a human (may be a technical or philosophical reason) or a reasoned argument that the brain is simply a machine, which, given sufficient research can be modelled in software or hardware

22. (a) (i) smaller number of neurons/perceptrons in artificial network

        (ii) given stimuli; "trainer" gives feedback on whether or not output was "correct"; an algorithm adjusts the weights linking the perceptrons; process repeated many times until the output is reliably correct

        (iii) any reasonable example eg financial modelling, handwriting recognition

        (iv) there is no algorithm, so it cannot be stated with complete certainty that the correct response will always be given (just like a human expert)

22. (b) (i) increased processor speed allows large amounts of data to be processed in real-time; increases in memory allow pattern-matching to be developed with large graphical data

        (ii) they can "see" and therefore identify the object on which they are working; they are less likely to damage other machines or humans if they can "see" them

        (iii) ability to learn (eg a welding robot might be able to develop its own set of moves in an industrial process)

Section III
Part B—Computer Networking

23. (a) modem, communications software
modem—convert digital signals to analogue suitable for telecoms
software—control the modem, encode data, manage flow of data between laptop and remote server

    (b) (i) laptop computer and remote server must be using same standards for sending and receiving data

        (ii) communication speed, size of data packet, start and stop bits

    (c) (i) Competition between newspapers for exclusive stories.

        (ii) Descriptions of data encryption, login with passwords, also"use of virtual private networks".

    (d) *Descriptions of two of*:
Higher speed of transfer;
Lower error rate;
different protocols in use

24. (a) (i) Router; accept gateway but not a bridge!!

        (ii) Internetwork; accept WAN
Note NOT intranet

    (b) TCP responsible for breaking file data into packets, verifying delivery, reassembling packets
IP responsible for delivery to correct network address, including routing if necessary

    (c) Leased line has higher bandwidth than ISDN but more expensive to lease. ISDN line rental less but call charges apply whenever it is used.
Leased line permanently available. ISDN would require one side "dial up" the other when communication has to take place.

    (d) (i) could be http or ftp

        (ii) **Advantages**
A single server would be easier to manage—software and data only have to be loaded to one site. Data is more likely to be up to date and accurate if there is only one copy in use at any one time.

24. (*d*) (ii) (cont.)

Disadvantages

Security of information, need a backup. Information not always available as server may have to be taken off line for servicing or updating of information. 3 clear points from either advantage/disadvantage

If cost mentioned, there must be reference to balance between capital and bandwidth

25. (*a*) (i) peer to peer network

(ii) Allow access only to named users—do not allow "guest" access.

(iii) Set access rights of shared folder to read only.

(*b*) (i) client-server network

(ii) server computer
server software at server, client software at each station

(*c*) (i) **data security**—all shared files on a single server which can be protected from unauthorised access by password or physically locking it away in a secure room. Users can be set up and access rights controlled centrally

data integrity—all shared data accessed from single server. Only one copy being used by all users therefore more likely to be correct and accurate

(ii) E-mail
Need a server to store mail for each mail user.

26. (*a*) Set parameters for communication—speed etc
Implement IP over telephone line (SLIP, PPP)

(*b*) Use search engine
Search for design notation **AND** software development (*Note must be complex search*)

(*c*) A—protocol, B—host name, C—file name/path to file

(*d*) The school may have a faster link—possible ISDN–to ISP
Gateway (proxy server) may cache files locally
Schools computers may render pages faster, giving appearance of faster downloads

(*e*) (i) Downloading of files may introduce virus to school network
To prevent breaches of copyright
Excessive use of bandwidth

(ii) Firewall

Section III
Part C—Computer Programming

27. (*a*) 2D array with 2 columns and 5 rows (in this example)
each row of the array holds the division result and the remainder
Could also be a 2D array with 5 columns and 2 rows where each column holds the division result and remainder

(*b*) The algorithm below is one possible answer. There may be other possible answers
iterate = 0 (lower array bound);
   while (decConvert <> 0)
      begin
         remainder = decConvert MOD 2
         decConvert = decConvert DIV 2;
         array[1][iterate] = decConvert;
         array[2][iterate] = remainder;
         add 1 to iterate
   end while
Key points—management of array pointer, allocation of values to array

Range of values which can be dealt with limited by size of array.

(*c*) (i) Either of the following descriptions

1. The array could be subdivided and values of the division held in one half which the remainders are held in the other. A fixed offset value would provide a paired matching.

OR

2. The two values could be held in adjacent array positions with each value pair offset in the array by adding 2 to the index position of the first pair value.
It would also be possible to use a 1D array of records

(ii) Any **TWO** of the following:
• the code to create the array and to traverse it would be more complex
• complexity leads to likelihood of more errors
• complexity makes it more difficult to debug
• complexity increases time required to maintain the code

28. (*a*) (i) ONE of: end of file, array bounds error, insufficient file access privileges, file does not exist
Not Div by zero!

Computing Higher 2001 (cont.)

28. (a) (ii) Variety of possibilities depending upon implementation. Must relate to error mentioned in (i)
eg use conditional loop to control reading from file,—so that end of array is detected.
test for end of file or array full conditions—so that reading is stopped (detect return code on attempt to open—report this).
detect error as an exception/through error trapping routine—report error.

(b) set position_array to 1;
loop while NOT EOF(textfile)
    begin
        read name and store in array1[position_array]
        read name and store mark in array2[position_array]
        increment position_array
    end loop

(c) (i) care has to be taken to sort corresponding values in both arrays

(ii) Would only require one array data structure. Clearer program task.

(d) (i) *TWO of*: that the array is not full already; the "top" of the existing data has not been reached; whether the new name is later in alphabetical order than the current item

(ii) Suitable diagram showing "bubbling" up of array elements "above" the insertion point

29. (a)

3	← Top
7	

(b) upper limit = 3

(c) if stack pointer ◇ upper limit then
    begin
        stack pointer = stack pointer + 1
        stack[stack pointer] = symbol
    end

(d) (i) stack overflow

(ii) by first checking that the stack pointer ◇ upper array bounds

(iii) the program could trap the error using the test given in (ii)
the program could report a stack overflow error

30. (a) *In these responses, head refers the point in the queue which will be processed next, tail to the last item entered into the queue. The queue is assumed to fill from the lower bound to the upper bound of the array. A basic queue implementation is assumed.*

(i) pointers to head and tail of queue (both required)

(ii) head pointer is 1 less than lower bound of array. Tail pointer is upper bound of array

(b) (i) Problem—due to upper bound condition—even when items dequeued, no way to add item to queue.

(ii) Either move items down in array, adjusting pointers OR implement circular queue, with modulo arithmetic to wrap round pointer values OR implement queue using eg linked list

(c) suitably labelled diagram showing the tail pointer being incremented and the head remaining static

(d) set pointer to head of queue
loop while pointer ◇ queue tail
    begin
        if username of queue[pointer] = searchitem then
            increment occurences
    increment pointer
    end loop

Section III
Part D—Multimedia Technology

31. (a) (i) an authoring tool is a program which helps you write hypertext or multimedia applications through the creation and manipulation of multimedia elements into a single presentation

(ii) *any two from*:
—links objects such as text, illustrations, sound;
—defines objects relationships to one another and sequences them in appropriate order;
—may support a scripting language for more sophisticated applications;
—buttons to control the flow of information, allow choices to be made, to initiate events
—menu selections to allow choice
—events which are inactive until the user initiates them
—navigation maps which allows different routes to different sources of information

31. (b) *Two points for each item, for example*
optical data storage—description of developments eg speed of disks and drives; CD-ROM to DVD allowing larger storage of data, hence allowing all elements of multimedia to be stored. Faster transfer of data.
sound card technologies—description of sound card developments eg development from single bleep sounds to 8 bit cards; stereo; CD quality 16 bit audio; wavetable sound; storing the waveform "signatures" of real musical instruments in the sound card's memory, then playing them back at varying pitch in order to reproduce different notes; current sound cards provide a MIDI interface (standard hardware and software protocol for allowing musical instruments to communicate with each other); many sound cards provide FM synthesis for backward compatibility with older cards and software.
Sound cards commonly use 8 or 16 bit samples at sampling rates from about 4000 to 44,000 samples per second.
The samples may also be contain one channel (mono) or two (stereo).
Most sound cards provide the capability of mixing, combining signals from different input sources; no longer dependent upon internal speakers. High quality stereo sound, playback of audio CDs and digitised sounds. Digital in/out capability therefore no loss in A to D conversion

(c) *accept any* **one** *description from*:
MIDI (.mid)—MIDI stands for Music Instruments Digital Interface; a standard for transmitting musical information between electronic instruments and computers; size of a MIDI file is small; quality of the music is very good
WAVE (.wav)—WAVE files are sound data-digital representation of an analog signal; linearly encoded; files can be large; can be stereo/mono 8/16 bit
UNLAW (.au)—the original NeXt machine sound standard. It is a digitised sound data file similar to WAVE files and takes a lot of storage space. Common on Unix/Sun platforms
MOD (.mod)—a collection of sample data and a description of how to play these samples in a certain order, pitch, and distortion on four channels; samples don't necessarily have to be from real musical instruments. The MOD format reveals a big advantage over the WAVE and MIDI formats. Any natural sound can be used as an instrument, where as MIDI can't do this. The size of a MOD file is much smaller compared to a WAVE file that produces the same sound.

31. (c) **AIFF (.aiff)**—The Audio Interchange File Format allows one program open a digital recording created by another program. The format actually used on CDs—though it can represent the encoded digitised sound at different sample rates and
SND(.snd)—An Amiga sound extension that is a sound data file
MP3—supported by many software applications, can be used for DVD, portable music players, web music. Compression ratio of the order of 10:1 compared to eg AIFF

32. (a) *any* **three** *from*:
—hierarchical structure of pages; number of pages; interaction and links;
—storyboard showing flow of presentation;
—list of hardware, software and media elements used
—order of multimedia elements
—number of different elements?
—consistent user response structures (dialog boxes etc)
—consistent navigation prompts (bars, arrows etc)
—error reporting
—background

(b) —most authoring packages are icon based and developer may need to perform an action which is not available in the menus; more complex tasks and accurate timing sequences may be obtained
—scripts may be "saved" and used in other presentations ie reusable code
—script based allows more flexibility for developers; Icon based may not offer the necessary tools required

(c) (i) *Any* **three** *of*:
image size; colour depth; frame rate/refresh rate/scan rate; brightness; resolution; display mechanism

(ii) video adapter card contains the circuitry which generates the signals for the appropriate video display; contains a certain amount of RAM (VRAM—buffers image data); better quality and larger images can be obtained by increasing VRAM available
most cards support 3D, have a good refresh rate, 32 bit + colour depth, high resolution, motion compensation

33. (a) (i) *description of characteristics from* bit depth, colour, resolution
bit depth—scanner records varying amounts of information about each pixel (more pixels = better quality). The amount of information that the scanner can remember about each pixel is commonly referred to as bit depth. A bit depth of 12 can identify 4,096 grey scales.

Computing Higher
2001 (cont.)

33. (a) (i) **Colour**—how "true to life" the digitised colours are for quality photographs or other images required

Resolution—measures how many pixels a scanner can assign to any given image or document. Most scanners start at about 300 × 300 dots/pixels per inch –r reads 90,000 pixels per square inch for the image being scanned

(ii) **handheld:** dragging scan head over the image; useful for scanning objects other than flat pages; poorer quality than flat bed; but less expensive

flatbed: operates like a photocopier; scan head moves over image; can accommodate paper sizes larger than A4 and large books and magazines

sheet fed: limited to A4 sheets; image is fed by mechanical rollers and scanned one line at a time until complete image has been processed

Characteristics in terms of
High resolution for graphic capture (OCR software—for text capture)
At least 36 bit colour depth—for photographs

(b) Answers **must** include descriptions. Other graphics formats are possible—
TIFF—is compressed format, therefore more economical in storage space; a common graphics format which is easily imported into WP and DTP packages; TIFF can handle monochrome, greyscale, 8 bit or 24 bit colour images
GIF—only allows 256 colours
JPEG—lossy compression (*allow detail loss*)
EPS—needs Postscript printer
BMP—less flexible

(c) *Really looking for the "advanced" image processing tasks as listed in the Arrangements with brief descriptions.*
*Therefore **three** of:*
Rotating, flipping, resizing, scaling, cropping, filling, morphing, Gamma correction image contrasting, outline sharpening
With description of the task carried out.

(d) Response should be a comparison, eg
ASCII—text will easily transfer to any application; however
RTF—will retain formatting features

34. (a) (i) description of MPEG/JPEG; lossy compression; eg compression of graphical data using MPEG where only the changes from one frame to another are stored instead of the entire frame **OR** description of RLE, Huffman or other "standard" data compression technique
ADPCM—Audio, only stores deltas so only 1/4 of storage required
AC-3—Audio, noise reduction used
MPEG—Video, only saves deltas between successive frames

(ii) any suitable description eg lossy compression technique for graphic or sound files; any situation where removal of some data would be acceptable and loss is not noticeable to the human ear and eye
non lossy for text data where loss of any data would be unacceptable

(b) *Description of any **two** from:*
Vector: WMF, PICT, EPS, CDR
Bitmapped: BMP, TIFF, GIF, PCX, JPEG
(+ any other acceptable answers)
with some description of characteristics of each named filetype eg
GIF—bitmapped, lossless compression, only 256 colours
BMP—bitmapped, Windows standard, large files
TIFF—bitmapped, mostly used for DTP, variable storage structure
JPEG—bitmapped, lossy compression, most commonly used format
CDR—vector, proprietary, used for Corel Graphics
EPS—vector, encapsulated postcript

(c) *Any **three** from:*
Blend—sharp edges on images blend into one another (colour graduations)
Smear—softens an image by smudging/ smearing darker areas of the image
Colour depth—increasing the colour depth retains all the image's colours, decreasing the colour depth may reduce the number of colours below that currently used by the image. Low colour depths = smaller file sizes
Colour palette—converts the logical colour numbers stored in each pixel of video memory into physical colours that can be displayed on the monitor. Changes to the palette affect the whole screen at once and can be used to produce special effects which would be much slower to produce by updating pixels. **Also allow** Scaling, resizing, filling, cropping, pixel editing, airbrush red-eye correction

Computing Higher
2002

Section I

1. (a) Fewer rules of arithmetic to be encoded in circuitry

   Less chance of signal degradation changing data

   Binary numbers easily represented using digital electronic devices

   Due to 2 states (1 and 0) this can easily be represented as 0 volts and some volts electronically

   (b) 11110010 or (ii)

2. (a) Each character is represented by a 7 bit **binary** number (accept 8 bit or 1 byte)

   (b) The complete list of all characters which a device **or the system** can handle

3. The instructions which control the processor are stored in memory along with the data which is to be processed—separate from the processing unit

   This means that the same processing unit can be used for many different tasks. Just change the program

4. (i) Software which controls and maintains the computer system

   (ii) Programs which **provide tools and functions** to enable the computer to carry out specific tasks for the user. eg wp, db etc

5. (a) (i) Processor speed, RAM. Backing Storage, Number of processors

   (ii) Server should have faster processor, more RAM, more backing storage space

   (b) Creating packets to be placed on the network, checking the address of incoming packets, encryption, Data Integrity, multi user access (user login, checking passwords, creating users and groups etc) *Any one*

6. To store data in transit between cpu and device to make up for difference in speed,

   To perform data conversion (eg difference in voltage, difference in data representation),

   Control signals, Provide status information, Recognition of device information

7. (a) *Any suitable response of the following type*
   - To fully explain the needs of the client
   - To fully specify the problem
   - To produce and agree a problem specification
   - To observe, clarify and model the current system

   (b) Requirements specification, operational requirements specification or problem specification

7. (c) **Corrective** maintenance is the changing of code to fix errors found after release of the software

   Adaptive maintenance is the amending of the program to cope with its new environment, (to remove clashes with other programs or to optimise for the OS)

   Perfective maintenance is the amending of the code to include new features and optimisations suggested by the users after release

8. (a) A module library contains a number of pre-written routines which the programmer can use within a program

   (b) **Two** *of the following responses*
   - Use of parameters
   - No global variables
   - Self-contained
   - Good documentation
   Any other valid

   (c) Robust software does not crash if invalid data is entered

   Software is fit for purpose if it matches the specification arrived at during the analysis phase in consultation with the client. It does the task as specified

9. Linear search

10. Features could be indentation of sub-clauses, blank lines between code blocks, capitalised/bold/colour keywords, line numbers

11. A clear description of the passing of the value of the variable into a module, where any changes do not affect the original value afterwards eg a second copy of variable is created to be used within the module, thus unaffecting the original

12. Syntax error is a grammar error eg PINT "Hello world!"

    This is introduced at implementation

    A logic error is introduced at the analysis or design phase and affects the algorithm eg LET months = years * 10

Section II

13. (a) **ALU**—carries out arithmetic and logical operations

    Control Unit—manages fetching, decoding and executing of instructions

    Registers—temporary storage areas

    (b) Set up address on address bus and open memory location

    Read line on control bus activated

    Data bus carries data from memory location to processor

    (c) Faster processors to enable instructions to be carried out quicker. Larger RAM to enable larger programs and data to be loaded at the same time. Wider data buses. Faster clock speeds. Caches.

Computing Higher
2002 (cont.)

13. (c)   (Although Parallel processing, RISC and pipelining are not explicit in the arrangements, they could be possible responses)

(d)   2^24 memory locations and 16 bits for each storage location
16777216 × 16 bits = 33554432 bytes = 32 Mb

14. (a)   **Pseudocode**—step by step algorithm written in English or
Flow chart—graphical breakdown of steps required

(b)   **Editor**—to create and amend the code—Implementation/testing/maintenance
Interpreter/compiler—to translate HLL into machine code Implementation/testing/maintenance
Debugger/error tracing—to find and identify errors—Implementation/testing/maintenance

(c)   Data types and structures required, operations required
User interface required, type of task (arithmetic, problem solving etc), what hardware is needed to support the program, typical end users, what environment will the program operate, the type of problem to be solved AND exemplification

(d)   Modular code, meaningful variable/procedural names, internal commentary, indentation

(e)   **Normal**—1·5, 2, 3 etc to test that the program works correctly (reliable and correct)
Boundary—0, 40 or 60 or 100 or 24 × 7 to test extremes
Exceptions—negative numbers, text to test that the program is robust and will not crash due to unexpected data

15. (a)   **WP**—to produce and edit text for the newsletter
Graphics—to edit pictures for the newsletter
DTP—to produce newsletter page layouts
DB—to maintain a database of members
SS—to keep club accounts
E-Mail client—to distribute newsletter electronically

(b)   Club members may have different hardware and/or software from club
Use of standard data formats will enable transfer data between different platforms

(c)   description of a validation check on any field in the database
could describe setting upper and lower limits when defining field or defining field as a list or drop down menu

15. (d)   recommend **either**, with any of the following advantages:
digital camera: pictures available immediately; direct production of digital image; no need to buy film or a separate camera
OR
scanner: cheaper than a digital camera; can scan existing photographs; can be used for other purposes eg OCR

(e)   (i)   a language which can be used to write programs (scripts) which control other applications or programs or are contained within an application

(ii)   could be used to write a macro (or script) to automate some process (eg a complex search/sort/layout process in the database)

16. (a)   file management, memory management, input/output, HCI, command interpretation, program scheduling
(allow any reasonable sub-functions of the above or descriptions of the above functions)

(b)   any *two* utilities eg virus checker, defragmenter, backup utility, sector editor, file repair utility

(c)   (i)   eg optical disc, DAT, zip drive, jaz drive

(ii)   eg
optical disc—allows files larger than 1·4 Mb to be saved on a portable device
DAT—allows fast backups to be made of the HD

(d)   (Prolog or lisp)—program consists of facts and rules rather than a coded algorithm

(e)   interpreter used during development as it allows easier editing and partial testing, errors more easily traced
compiler used to produce runnable machine code final version, faster execution

17. (a)   Improves readability, aids maintenance, splits up problem into manageable sections, can allocate modules to members of team

(b)   Makes the procedure more flexible, or re-usable

(c)   (i)   Less memory used to store integers, arithmetic more accurate, integers can be processed faster

(ii)   Array of integers

(d)   eg
If grade > = upper_grade AND grade < = lower_grade

(e)   A conditional loop eg REPEAT or WHILE
loop until grade = sentinel_value
     get grade
     if grade not sentinel_value then
         process grade
     end if
end of loop   or similar

18. (a) Consistency of input screens, use of on-line help, meaningful error messages, other valid answers

(b) **Position of maximum**—integer passed by reference
accident array—array of integer passed by reference

(c) A loop variable. Prevents the possibility of accidentally changing another variable with same name in other part of program. Local variable could also be used to store maximum value—*other answers are possible*

(d) (i) fixed loop, if structure

(ii) loop for current_position = 1 to 6 (or number_of_areas)
      if number at current_position > number at position_of_current_ maximum   then
      set position_of_current_ maximum to current_position
end of loop
other answers possible

Section III
Part A—Artificial Intelligence

19. (a) (i) She is the Knowledge Engineer

(ii) Dr Ridge is not an expert in bats and has to work with Tony to make sure that the finished system has the correct information. Tony is not familiar with the construction of computer programs.

(b) **Knowledge Base**—The list of facts and rules comprising the total information known by the system
Inference Engine—The mechanism by which the system chooses the fact or rule to apply to solve any given query. It employs pattern matching of the goals and sub-goals to the rules and facts in the knowledge base

(c) (i) **one**, *or more, of the following points*
   • A list of sub-goals satisfied which has led to the response given
   • A description of the reasons for the system suggesting this particular answer
   • Explanation of **how** a solution was found or **why** a question is being asked

(ii) linking to the fact that BatSearch is a training program eg will help user to understand what the important factors are in identifying bats so that they can learn how to do this themselves

(iii) There is a legal requirement that bat handlers are licensed. If someone were trained by the expert system they might think that they had been given permission to handle bats. The law might consider the system to be partly responsible for this infringement

19. (d) Testing: to provide suitable test data. **Only domain experts has enough knowledge to test program**
Documentation: to check details of the information ie legal statement
Maintenance (Perfective)—any further developments volunteers need to know

20. (a) (i) "true" or "yes"

(ii) Goal **sentence**(badger meets otter) is matched at 10
Sub goal noun(badger) matched at 1
Sub goal verb(meets) matched at 6
Sub goal noun(otter) matched at 3
All three sub goals are true
Therefore goal is true

(b) (i) A = badger, C = fox

(ii) A clear description of the addition of a fourth sub-goal of the form **and not (A = C)**. (Allow various symbols for not equal to)

(c)

Complex sentence(A B C D E)	if	adjective (A)
	and	noun(B)
	and	verb(C)
	and	adjective(D)
	and	noun(E)

(d) Answers should comment fully upon both of the following:
• Greatly increased number of **facts** for the system to deal with to represent all possible words
• Greater number of **rules** to express the variety of legal sentence structures

Alternative answers may comment upon the **technical** difficulties. These should make reference to the greatly increased memory/processor requirements

21. (a) Depth first follows one branch to its end before trying another branch.
Breadth first tests all nodes at one level before moving to next level.
use of memory to store previous successes is greater in breadth first, breadth first will find the best solution, depth first may go down a branch where there is no solution

(b) (i) This is a "rule of thumb" or supposition which directs the system towards where the solution is likely to be

(ii) The heuristic allows the size of the search space to be reduced. This will greatly decrease the time for finding the solution, as less of the tree will be traversed

Computing Higher
2002 (cont.)

21. (c) (i) response should make a clear
connection between visual recognition
systems and the manufacturing context
eg
   - Allows robots arms to check
     orientation of components
   - Allows boards to be visually checked
     and rejected by system
   - Reduction in the number of wasted
     components if checking done
     automatically at each stage

(ii) formal connection between the above
points and a saving in time or cost eg
less waste leads to reductions in costs—
possible increase in profit

(d) **Procedural:**
Advantage—common language, many
trained programmers, etc
Disadvantage—not so easy to model
decision making process

Declarative:
Positive—suited to pattern matching/
problem solving, uncertainty okay
Negative—requires specialist programmers

22. (a) • these are numeric values of probability
attached to facts
   • they range between 0, for definitely false,
   and 1 for definitely true (or 0% to 100%)

(b) (i) A clear description of a diagnosis or
process control application which
includes **explicit** reference to certainty
factors. **Must explain why advice is
not definitive in this area**

(ii) Poor advice from system may lead to
loss of money or physical harm to
users (or users' clients). This may lead
to legal action against developers.
Users should be warned against using
this advice exclusively. Disclaimers
added to software

(c) This is a very wide area, which could
include:
   • Better storage media, which can store
   larger knowledge bases and access them
   faster
   • Cheaper, faster RAM—more of the search
   tree held in memory, therefore "shortest
   path" optimisations can take place
   • Digital optics—visual recognition systems
   etc
   • Faster processors—larger throughput

22. (d) The ability to recognise (or identify)
individual objects in a picture from a huge
range of angles using colour, shading and
prior experience
The ability to extrapolate 3D information
from a 2D scene
Automatic adjustment to light
Depth perception
Concavity/convexity

(e) • Inner layers of the net changing weighting
values to reflect new knowledge
   • Training and feedback changes weightings
   therefore improving knowledge

Section III
Part B—Computer Networking

23. (a) **Economic factor**—reduced comms costs/
shared access to expensive equipment/
geographic spread of organisations/
competition/demand for up to date info
Technical factor—advances in computer
technology **with exemplification**/new data
transmission media and methods/
international standards/improved software/
Internet technology

(b) (i) print server, communications server,
applications server, e-mail server, proxy
server, CD server

(ii) print server—stores, and processes
print jobs
comms server—manages
communications across the network
e-mail server—holds mail prior to
delivery (store and forward) etc

(c) It is client-server as a peer-peer network
does not have dedicated servers

(d) user files are stored on the file server's HD
accept encryption if linked to **transmission**
of data
user must log on using user ID and password
network OS checks this and only allows user
to access appropriate files

(e) (i) all user files are stored centrally, and so
copies need to be kept in case they are
corrupted in any way

(ii) suitable backing store (probably a tape
drive), with automatic backup schedule
(eg every 24 hours at midnight)

24. (a) (i) **repeater**—boosts signal where
distance between nodes causes
deterioration

(ii) **bridge**—connects 2 networks using the
same protocol

(iii) **router**—connects networks in an
internet work, sends packets of data
towards the correct destination

(b) (i) **FTP**—allows files to be transferred
between nodes on a network
SMTP—controls the routing of e-mails
across a network

24. (b) (ii) allows networks throughout the world of many types to communicate so long as they all use the same protocols

(c) www.billtheplumber.co.uk
+ more recognisable/memorable: clearly indicates a UK-based company
− cost of domain registration, lack of availability of domain name
www.freewebservices.com/users/pages/billtheplumber
+ probably free
− clumsy, difficult to remember name

(d) (i) eg internet allows "Bill" to advertise widely; on-line enquiries

(ii) small company might not be able to afford to set up internet advertising, lack of expertise regular checking of feedback (e-mail) and/or web design (extra employee to pay perhaps?)

25. (a) shared access to printers
shared access to software/databases

(b) network interface card (eg ethernet card) to allow connection to network
network OS to allow communication with the network or NIC driver

(c) (i) easier to extend/alter or failure of 1 cable only affects one station

(ii) a hub or switch to which all computers are connected at the centre of star

(iii) 1 mark for **two** types—UTP (twisted pair, cat 5), Coax or fibre optic, UTP—Cheap, easy to install, fibre optic—higher bandwidth, less signal degradation Coax—cheap, reliable over short distances

(d) (i) an internetwork is 2 or more LANs connected to each other

(ii) library users have access to software on school network
school pupils have access to public library databases
OR school pupils could access school network from library in the evening

26. (a) (i) LAN has higher bandwidth

(ii) LAN mainly uses coaxial cable or UTP (fibre also possible)
WAN uses trunk phone lines, satellite link, microwave link, fibre optic cable

(b) encryption of data; use of dedicated fibre optic cable
passwords not acceptable

(c) (i) 24 hour access using ATMs or Internet access or many different banks can be accessed other than one that holds account

(ii) less need for manual counting/processing of money or paperwork

26. (d) (i) video conferencing or video phone

(ii) need high speed modem, ISDN, cable modem, broadband or ADSL, webcam and video conferencing software

Section III
Part C—Computer Programming

27. (a) (i) The list must be sorted

(ii) Binary search compares search item with item at middle of list in order to restrict further search. This only works if list is in order

(b) variable to store position of top of sub list, variable to store position of bottom of sub list, variable to store position of middle of sub list, variable to store search item middle is calculated from top and bottom, search item is compared with item at middle of list if search item is **smaller than the** item **at the middle of the** list then the contents of **top** variable are **set** to the **middle** variable −1
If greater than middle then bottom is set to middle +1
The middle is then re-calculated to start new search

(c) Binary Search : 2 Comparisons
Linear Search : 4 Comparisons

(d) When item to be searched for is first in list. Linear Search required 1 comparison—Binary Search requires 3 comparisons. Also short list as time is saved by not sorting

(e) A palmtop has limited storage and processing power

28. (a) (i) string array with 13 elements

(ii) *Any **two** of the following*:
more readable than 13 variables
ease of parameter passing
assists modularity
any other valid reason

(b) **Stack**—list/array where new items are pushed onto end of list and items popped from same end—operates under LIFO
Queue—list/array where items pushed onto end of list and items removed from head—operates under FIFO

(c)
• If card > 0 then   If there are any cards in the stack
• Let card$ = bank$(card)   record the top card
• Let card = card − 1   decrement the stack pointer

(d) Open (channel to) file
For member = 1 to 13 **or 1 to max**
    Write bank$(member) to file
End loop
Close (channel to) file

Computing Higher
2002 (cont.)

29. (a) *any 2 from:*

create file—to create a new file to receive the data
open file to write—to prepare the file to accept new data
append to file—to add a competitor's results to those already there
close file—to close the file when no further data is to be added
read from file—to retrieve the data for further processing

(b) record of:
name: string
bibno: integer
time: real
penalty: integer

(c) (i) any sort algorithm (likely answers will be selection, exchange (**bubble**), selection-exchange, quicksort)

(ii) accept answer as a description, a diagram showing an example list after each pass, or as pseudocode
[*see www.cs.brockport.edu/cs/javasort.html for examples of algorithms*]

(d) (i) eg selection sort: double size of list, selection exchange: just size of list

(ii) eg selection sort n(n–1) comparisons, selection exchange n(n–1)/2 comparisons

(e) these are all "normal" data; full testing would have to include extreme/exceptional data

30. (a) Rainfall: array (1..20,1..12) of real or array (1..12,1..20)

(b) (i)

Algorithm or example of programming code eg:

```
count_months = 0
for i=1 to 12 do
    if rainfall(year,i) > 10.0 then
        count_months: = count_months + 1
    endif
endfor

set count for months to 0
repeat for each month i
    if rainfall(year,i) > 10.0 then
        add 1 to count for months
    endif
until months = 12
```

(ii) identify the correct loop structure (nested for) correct condition (if rainfall(j.i) > 10.0)

30. (c)
```
for i=1 to 20 do
    max_month(i):=rainfall(i,l)
    for j=2 to 12 do
        if rainfall(i,j) > max_month(i) then
            max_month(i):=rainfall(i.j):
        endif
    endfor
endfor
```

(d) Marks must only be given for specific program changes
reference to changing array dimensions (dim array for 40 instead of 20)
reference to changing nested loops (First loop changes to 1 to 40 instead of 1 to 20)

Section III
Part D—Multimedia Technology

31. (a) (i) Rapid navigation can be used through cards, pages etc
Objects can be linked together
Navigation using hyperlinks
The ability to save results for later use
Good browsing capabilities

(ii) The ability to **link** media objects such as sound, video, graphics etc

(b) (i) Staff training, typing tutors, assessment, distance learning

(ii) Users can work at own pace, changing of direction, stopping for breaks, tally of scores given, learning at home instead of workplace

(c) (i) DVD has higher storage capacity than CD-ROM – 4·7 to 17 Gb compared with 300 Mb to 850 Mb
This means that more media elements can be stored, thus improving presentation
It could also mean that higher quality media elements can be stored eg higher resolution, full screen video, higher frame rate etc

(ii) 1 mark for each appropriate development with appropriate explanation:
Colour depth—millions of colours are now available
Resolution—better quality images
Refresh rate—faster, no flickering apparent to human eye
Brightness/contrast—ability to make images appear brighter or duller

(iii) **Faster Processor**—allows programs to be loaded more quickly, calculations performed more quickly—smoother animation, faster navigation
More RAM—allows more programs and data to be loaded at any one time, leads to better quality video playback, full screen rather than small window

32. (a) Storyboard—design of each page/stage/card of multimedia presentation
Allows designer to have a clear plan of navigation routes, where multimedia elements will be positioned, how each page will be linked to another etc

(b) **Icon based**—use of preprogrammed buttons, icons, menus which can be used to create program. Easier coding
Faster implementation, don't need programming skills
OR
Script—more flexibility with multimedia elements, more control with navigation

(c) Scanner to input logo
Video camera—to capture frames
Video capture card—to input frames onto a computer system
Video adapter card—to allow video to be viewed on the display device

(d) Responses should include input, process and output of sound:
Sound card required for whole process (I, O and P)
Input—microphone
Process—sound manipulation software or name (Quicktime, Win Decks, Wave Studio, Waveshaper etc) **or** authoring package (Hyperstudio, Director etc)
Output—speakers (for amplification)

(e) Minimum MPC standards allow devices to be compliant with multimedia components. Allows all devices, interfaces to work together. Minimum hardware requirements for computer to be classified as a multimedia machine

33. (a) *for 2 devices from:*
scanner, digital camera, video camera
Scanner—picture taken by "normal" camera and scanned into the computer
Digital camera/video camera—photos taken and camera connected directly to computer for input

(b) (i) **Lossy**—compression leads to loss of information. When image is decompressed it will have less detail than original. This may still be acceptable to the human eye
Lossless—compression technique manages to encode all information so that when the image is decompressed it is exactly the same as the original. No detail is lost

(ii) **JPEG (JPG)**—millions of colours available, common format
GIF—common format, lossless compression so original file stored
TIFF—any number of colours and options available
PNG, BMP

33. (c) **Filling**—adding colours to image
Pixel editing—to remove scratches by changing colour of individual pixels
Cloning stamp—to remove scratches/blemishes/unwanted images by changing colour of pixels using another area of pixels
Special effects such as vignetting
Removing red eye, scaling, resizing, cropping and descriptions

(d) The ability to move text and graphics freely about a page with ease
DTP packages allow graphics from a wide area of formats including TIFFs
Text Wrap—text to flow around graphics
Master pages—items on the master page will appear on all pages
Non-printing guides—to help with alignment of text and graphics

34. (a) MIDI allows for music data to be passed in both directions from the keyboard to the computer
It is a standard for musical data so that data can be passed between devices made by different manufacturers

(b) **Frequency Modulation**—sounds are generated by combining and modifying the outputs of signal generators (oscillators)
Wave Table—Digitised sound samples are stored in a table of waveforms and played at different speeds to produce different notes.

(c) (i) **Compression**—the ability to achieve a smaller file size to "shrink" files
Sampling rate—how many amplitudes are captured per second, frequency of sound readings

(ii) *accept any* **one** *description from:*
MIDI (.mid)—MIDI stands for Music Instruments Digital Interface; a standard for transmitting musical information between electronic instruments and computers; size of a MIDI file is small; quality of the music is very good
WAVE (.wav)—WAVE files are sound data-digital representation of an analog signal; linearly encoded; files can be large; can be stereo/mono 8/16 bit
UNLAW (.au)—the original NeXt machine sound standard. It is a digitised sound data file similar to WAVE files and takes a lot of storage space. Common on Unix/Sun platforms

Computing Higher
2002 (cont.)

34. (c) (ii) **MOD (.mod)**—a collection of sample data and a description of how to play these samples in a certain order, pitch, and distortion on four channels; samples don't necessarily have to be from real musical instruments. The MOD format reveals a big advantage over the WAVE and MIDI formats. Any natural sound can be used as an instrument, where as MIDI can't do this. The size of a MOD file is much smaller compared to a WAVE file that produces the same sound.
AIFF (.aiff)—The Audio Interchange File Format allows one program to open a digital recording created by another program. The format actually used on CDs—though it can represent the encoded digitised sound at different sample rates.
SND (.snd)—An Amiga sound extension that is a sound data file
MP3—supported by many software applications, can be used for DVD, portable music players, web music. Compression ratio of the order of 10:1 compared to eg AIFF

(iii) **Low**—many amplitudes lost and the sound quality will be poor, not smooth and sharp
High—giant series of amplitudes taken, redundant information could be stored and hence wastage of storage space

Computing Higher
2003

SECTION I

1. Corrective – to correct errors which were not detected during testing.
Perfective – to add new features (functions) to the software.
Adaptive – to update the software to enable it to work in a new environment e.g. new OS.

2. correct – meets the specification (or fit for purpose)
reliable – how well the software operates without stopping due to design and coding faults / produces expected results at all times

3. (a) (i) structure chart, pseudocode, flowchart or any other known method

(ii) All are language independent, allow translation to different languages.
• Pseudocode useful for showing logic of single module
• structure diagram uses linked boxes showing hierarchy or shaped boxes to show constructs of program so is useful for showing overall structure and data flow
• flowchart uses shaped boxes to show constructs in the program and links to show sequence
• Pseudocode has line to line mapping with HLL – easy to convert to code

(b) Technical and user guides:
Technical
how to install software
installation requirements
User
how to operate the software, e.g. explanation of demands
tutorial guide

4. (a) Description of REPEAT or WHILE.

(b) Fixed loop is used when the number of iterations is known
Fixed loop will repeat a block of code for a fixed number of iterations

(c) repeating a section of code over again

5. (a) readable code is more easily understood by other programmers
or same programmer may be maintaining at a later date

(b) Any two from:
internal documentation/commentary
meaningful variable names
structured listings/indentation/white space
modularity

6. (a) Data bus width

   (b) An increase in word size increases system performance because more data can be processed in one cycle

7. Any two from:
   signal a read
   signal write
   reset processor registers
   interrupt current process
   carry clock signal

8. Order of objects could be changed
   Individual objects can be resized
   Individual objects can be moved/edited
   Objects can be resized with no loss of quality

9. rules of arithmetic are supported
   two values for 0 do not exist

10. (a) (i) bus, star, ring etc

    (ii) Below is a diagram of bus network topology

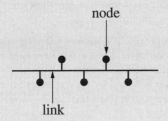

    (b) Answers depend on the topology diagram given above but could include:
        Bus – no communication can take place.
        Ring – no communication can take place
        Star – only one node is isolated

11. similarity: both are high level languages, both use modularity, both use data structures, both use control structures

    difference: scripting languages are embedded within an application or OS, procedural languages stand alone

12. (a) Resolution: number of dots per inch or number of pixels used to store image
        Capacity: amount of memory in the camera / number of pictures which can be stored.

    (b) The higher the resolution the more memory required to store one picture so fewer pictures can be stored / capacity will need to be increased

13. Word processing: RTF, text, ASCII
    Database: DBF, CSV, TAB separated
    Spreadsheet: SYLK, CSV, TAB separated
    Graphics: TIFF, JPEG, BMP, GIF
    Audio: MP3, WAV
    Web design: html
    Video editing: MPEG

SECTION II

14. (a) (i) Each memory location has a unique address.

    (ii) It stores the layout of memory indicating which addresses store the OS, programs and data and keeps each process separate so that overwriting does not occur.

    (b) (i) If data is stored in registers within the processor then less fetches to memory are required for a process.

    (ii) ALU – Adds/subtracts binary numbers. Performs logical AND, OR NOT etc.
        Control Unit – manages fetching, decoding and executing of instructions

    (c) (i) Contents of ROM cannot be changed.

    (ii) EPROMs or EEPROMs could be used which would allow data to be erased and rewritten OR Upgraded program can be stored on new ROM chip to be inserted into machine

    (iii) Advantage – Needs less power and circuitry is simpler
        Disadvantage – Needs continuous signal to refresh contents of chip
        Slower than SRAM

    (d) 2^{32} x 24 bits
        ÷8÷1024÷1024÷1024 = 12Gb
        12Gb – 1Gb = 11Gb

15. (a) One possible answer could include:
        Interview employees of agency, examine current paperwork, observe work place, questionnaires

    (b) Answers could include any two from:
        • easier to pass as a single parameter between code blocks
        • easier to read/understand code than if large number of variables used
        • easier to carry out list operations (search, sort etc)

    (c) (i) Pass by reference is where the location/address of the variable is passed to the code block. This enables changes to the variable contents to be made and passed back out.
        Pass by value is where the current value of the variable is passed into the code block, subsequent changes to that value do not affect the original variable.

    (ii) Pass by value as the search item should not be able to be changed.

    (d) All the job characteristics could be stored as facts and rules
        Then the applicant's attributes could be pattern matched against the facts stored to search for the best match i.e. querying facility is "built in".

Computing Higher
2003 (cont.)

15. (e) <u>Implementation</u>: When software is being upgraded, future programmers will have full description of how the code evolved. The function of the component parts will be clear

<u>Testing</u>: Corrective maintenance is the resolution of errors not discovered at the testing stage. Documentation (e.g. test data which was used) may help to identify areas where testing was inadequate.

16. (a) DTP, Word processor with graphics capability, Integrated package
Package must allow inclusion and manipulation of text and graphics

(b) (i) Bit depth – the number of bits used to represent the colour of a pixel, which defines the number of colours available
Type of interface – USB, parallel etc
Size of scanner surace (A3, A4, handheld etc) Scanning speed

(ii) 6 x 4 x 600 x 600 x 8 bits
(69 120 000 bits or 8 640 000 bytes)
÷8÷1024÷1024 = 8.24 Mb

(c) (i) Laptop – Larger RAM (128Mb) or faster processor which means more powerful applications (e.g. fully featured WP) can be used
OR larger backing storage (20Gb) so larger files/more powerful applications can be saved.
OR modem available so stories can be e-mailed to newspaper

Palmtop – handwriting recognition software (pen-based device) used for fast input, PCMCIA slots for attaching eg modem or memory cards OR physical size allows easy portability

(ii) Laptop – GUI (WIMP) system. Trackpad or trackerball can be used so easy to point and click. Standard keyboard useful when (large) stories have to be entered quickly.

Palmtop – Handwriting recognition. Easy to write notes quickly (interviews, comments etc.)

(d) <u>Advantage</u>: No need to create interface or searching engine, just create files, less coding required.

<u>Disadvantage</u>: Lack of control over "look and feel". Lack of control over searching algorithm.

17. (a) The operating system manages and maintains the computer system. O.S. provides link between applications and hardware.

17. (b) Utilities are programs that aid in the maintenance of (or enhance the use of) computer systems.
Disk formatter – formats media for use with OS
Defragmentation software – moves data around disk until it is stored in consecutive sectors
Virus checker – checks software for relevant viruses and feeds back to user

(c) So that data elements can be used by different computers and software.

(d) Large backing storage (Hard disc)/10GB+ – to ensure storage of OS
High processing power 500MHz+ – to ensure computer runs fast enough when carrying out other tasks.

(e) (i) The program is split into appropriate units therefore it is easier for the programmer to find relevant parts of the OS which are linked to the new features
OR
the new code could be tried and tested on its own.
OR
Different programmers can work on different modules

(ii) Test data which 'exercises' all program paths and special cases. All 3 types of test data must be mentioned.
Program is tested by typical users for real world exposure (beta testing)

18. (a) Robustness: A is more error prone as user may mistype the name, B – invalid entries not possible
Ease of data entry: A requires keyboard skills, B is able to be used by people with poor computer skills because no keyboard skills would be needed
Efficiency of Resources: A is not memory or processor intensive, B uses more memory/processor power to draw the menus etc

(b) • standard routines for the creation of buttons
• linking of buttons to segments of code
• any other valid point

(c) • use of subroutines to allow easier conversion
• sparse or no use of processor specific code
• use of different compilers to create different versions of object code
• meaningful variable names to allow conversion

(d) A module library is a set of pre-written routines which can be re-used
Module components have already been pre-tested

(e) set occurrences = 0
FOR position = 1 to maxarray
IF tree$(position) = target$
THEN increment occurrences
NEXT position
Display occurrences
(REPEAT could be used instead of FOR)

19. (a) (i) Global: variables which can be used by any part of the program.
Local: scope of the variable is limited to the procedure in which it is used

   (ii) Local variables cannot be accidentally changed by other parts of the software. Their use makes the behaviour of the code more predictable.

   (b) Any three from:
   • intended platform for software
   • suitability of type ie Prolog in AI application, assembler etc
   • data types available in language
   • features/constructs within language
   • support tools available i.e. CASE
   • any other valid point

   (c) array of strings
   Or string array or (2D) array of char.

   (d) set position to 0
   set current position to 1
   loop until end of list OR position >0
   if name at current position = window name
   set position to current position
   end if
   add 1 to current position
   end loop

   (e) An example of a possible answer is:
   Input/Output subsystem will take mouse clicks and pass data to a relevant part of the program

SECTION III – PART A Artificial Intelligence

20. (a) (i) Parallel processing allows several clauses or rules to be processed simultaneously so improving overall processing time.
Improvements to backing storage have meant that more information could be included in the knowledge base.
Improvements to internal memory have meant that larger knowledge bases can be manipulated.
Faster clock speeds have improved processing time so more could be expected from MYCIN.

   (ii) Any actions taken as a result of using the expert systems are at the users risk.

   A good explanatory interface will give justification of how a result is obtained and will help the user to evaluate the worth of the advice.

   (iii) Many copies of the expert system can be made and distributed, rather than just the few human experts.
   Expert not always at the point of need.
   Advice is always consistent whereas human experts may be inconsistent
   Combines knowledge of many experts.
   Can be used in training to confirm learner's knowledge.
   MYCIN does not forget things.

20. (b) Concept of knowledge engineer going back to domain expert for clarification / more information / checking etc after first consultation in order to proceed with the development of the system
OR
Different domain experts may give conflicting advice so need to go back to confirm advice

   (c) Many definitions of AI (or many types of intelligent behaviour) and each gives rise to a particular field of research.

   Also idea that it is easier to focus on making a machine (or application) which can perform a specific (AI) task than it is to create a "thinking machine".

21. (a) (i) No or false

   (ii) There is no information about Macdonald so to take the result that Macdonald is male is misleading.

   (b) Establish a match for female(friedland) at line 12,
   try to establish sub-goal male(friedland)
   subgoal fails
   so not(male(friedland)) succeeds

   (c) boss(grainger,W) AND female(W)

   (d) same_department(X,Y) if is_manager_of(Z,X) and is_manager_of(Z,Y)

   (e) (i) Recursion in line 14 needs a terminating condition which is provided by line 13.

   (ii) If lines 13 and 14 are the other way around the terminator would not be encountered by the search so the recursion would go on forever.

22. (a) Reasons could include:
a limited number of simple rules which were straight forward to code
limited computer technology meant anything more complicated would give processing / memory problems
game playing requires intelligence by people so was a good beginning for computer emulation (mixture of reasoning and creativity)

   (b) Computer may be programmed to follow strategies like a human player (use of heuristics).
   Computer may be programmed to learn from mistakes like a human player.
   Human player may not be very good at the game and so may play randomly like a poorly programmed computer.

   (c) (i) Pieces need to be turned right way up
   Detail must not be 'lost' in cutting of the jig-saw
   'Picture' for comparison needs to be a full size identical copy
   Position of camera
   Camera angle

Computing Higher
2003 (cont.)

22. (c)(ii) Identification of corners first and then edges...
to give a smaller number of pieces to search
to build up framework of jig-saw
OR group like coloured pieces and join groups together.

(d) Computer vision (linked to pattern matching) is needed for reduction of wastage, adaptability in jobs, freedom of mobility
Parallel processing to improve speed of processing of instructions

23. (a) Databases have rigid structure (records), facts and rules in knowledge bases are less well defined.
Databases produce results to simple/complex searches whilst the logic applied to a knowledge base allows for deductions to be made.

(b) Logic processes are independent of subject content of knowledge base
OR
single inference engine can be used with different knowledge bases

(c) Knowledge engineer – organises the knowledge of the expert into a form suitable for computer processing.

(d)(i) A certainty factor is a number which is attached to an advice rule to reflect degree of belief that advice, based on information provided, is correct

(ii) More than one alternative piece of advice, each with a certainty factor can be offered
Answers may also give a description of a particular situation involving several advice rules with certainty factors from any expert system shell

(e)(i) Examples:
Forward chaining:
IF hair IS brown AND
Face shape IS oval AND
Eye colour IS blue
THEN name IS Jenny

Backward chaining:
ADVISE name IS Jenny IF
Hair IS brown AND
Face shape IS oval AND
Eye colour IS blue

(ii) Forward chaining: prognosis, monitoring or control systems
planning + classification

(iii) Backward chaining: diagnostic problems, giving advice

SECTION III Part B - Computer Networking

24. (a)(i) peer-to-peer: each station on the network has the same status and can share files.
client-server: only certain computers on the network can make resources available to other stations.

(ii) All shared files stored on a central server means data more likely to be up to date and correct – everyone using the same data.
The security (access rights) of a central server can be controlled centrally so files are more secure.
Easier to backup centrally stored files.

(b) Telephone link uses modem which is slower (lower band width) than internal ethernet / communication channels.
Home computer less powerful than company computers.

(c) firewall computer is a security device to prevent unauthorised access (hacking) into a network
e.g.
• a firewall computer will only transfer packets for particular ports.
• a firewall computer may accept / reject packets from certain IP addresses

(d) A hacker who discovers a user's password cannot dial in from another telephone number.
Links can only be made to specific numbers.
Data is safer as it is guaranteed to be delivered to a private address.
User does not pay for telephone call.

25. (a)(i) Router

(ii) determines most efficient path for sending message to ultimate destination
bridges can't connect geographically distant networks, routers work with phone line or ISDN
all of the LANs are using TCP/IP

(b) TCP breaks down the data into packets and adds header(s)
IP delivers to receiver
TCP re-assembles packets in correct order.

(c) Large bandwidth, large buffering capacity to cope with size of sound and video files.

(d) Can queue jobs and deal with them by priority
Can direct print jobs to particular printers
Can store print jobs until they are printed.

(e)• Standard protocol which enables communication between different platforms
• works with whatever network cabling is already installed in the building
• isn't tied to one particular hardware or software vendor
• can be used on LAN to create private internet i.e. use of e-mail, browsers on LAN.

26. (a) Computer networks give access to large amounts of shared information.
Individuals or societies who do not have access to computer networks will not have the same access to information and so will be information poor.

(b) Different laws in different countries makes it hard for authorities to work together
Which country's law should be used—the one where the user is or the one where the host computer is?

(c) (i) protocol – method used to transfer resource e.g. ftp, http, mail
host_address – address of computer which holds the resource
resource name – file name or pathname of resource on the host computer

(ii) e.g. http://www.anyhost.com/news/index.html
protocol – http,
host_address – www.anyhost.com,
resource name – /news/index.html

(d) (i) circuit switching

(ii) packets broken down into the same size enables efficient storage management, allows the small packet to be sent by whatever route is convenient at the time, so that transmission appears to be quicker, other messages can be inserted when there are any gaps in transmission of small packets.

27. (a) (i) modem and communications software

(ii) software – controls modem, encodes data, manages data flow

(b) (i) Real time audio and visual communication of several people in different places anywhere with network connection, whiteboard utility allows greater interactivity.

(ii) By encrypting the signal on the network.

(c) (i) JPEG or any other acceptable, e.g. TIFF, GIF, PNG

(ii) JPEG compressed file format able to represent large range of colours and resolutions.
GIF – lossless compression

(d) Any two layers from:
• Physical layer: addresses physical characteristics of the network, e.g. cabling, connectors etc
• Data link layer: addresses size of packet, means of addressing packet, preventing two nodes transmitting at same time
• Network layer: routes packets from one network to another
• Transport layer: gives each node unique address, manages connections between nodes
• Session layer: makes sure sessions are established and maintained

27. (d) • Presentation layer: converts data sent over network from one type of representation to another, e.g. apply and remove compression
• Application layer: techniques that application programs use to communicate with the network, network OS works within this layer

Section III Part C – Computer Programming

28. (a) Array of integers

(b) current top of stack/stack pointer
the maximum size of the array

(c) Diagram or explanation should show:
• the array as a group of contiguous storage locations
• pointer to the last item of the list (top)
• space for adding the new item beyond
• incrementing the pointer to the new end item (top=top+1)
• the new item placed at the end (array(top)=new item)

(d) (i)
```
FOR current = 1 to (arraymax-1)
FOR count = (current+1) to arraymax
IF array(current) > array(count) THEN
let dummy = array(current)
let array(current) = array(count)
let array(count) = dummy
END IF
NEXT
NEXT (Many other algorithms are possible.)
```

(ii) Selection sort
uses a second array of same size therefore doubles memory requirement (2n locations) repeatedly finds the smallest item in the list and copies it into the current position (n squared)
Exchange sort
memory efficient (uses n + 1 locations) compares current element with rest of list, swapping smaller items into current. Then applies same to rest of list (n squared – n)

29. (a) (i) Array subscript error (reading past end of file is also acceptable)

(ii) Use a conditional loop which detects the end of the file and/or array

(b)
```
set count = 1
WHILE NOT end of data AND count <= arraymax
READ name$(count),hours(count)
count = count + 1
LOOP
```

(c) Using the following code example for illustrative purposes:
```
FOR count = 1 TO 1000
PRINT count; "squared is";count*count
NEXT count
```

Computing Higher
2003 (cont.)

29. (c) Compiler
All three lines are decoded once then the resultant object code is executed ie the print line is decoded once and executed 1000 times

Interpreter
All three lines are decoded then executed in turn ie the print line is decoded and executed 1000 times. This is 999 more translations of the print line.

(d) Note: This section shuffles up the remaining elements in both arrays and blanks the last item in the lists

```
FOR count = position to maxarray-1
name$(count) = name$(count+1)
hours(count) = hours(count+1)
NEXT count
name$(maxarray) = ""
hours(maxarray) = 0
maxarray = maxarray - 1
```

30. (a) Counting Occurrences (Conditional Loop and Count are also acceptable)

(b) Dry run is the manual execution of code using pen, paper and structured test data
Carried out to check the logic of code block

(c) This allows the modules to be incorporated into the program as "black boxes", much in the same way as modules in a library
Testing can be carried out by more than one programmer

(d) Trace tables:
Table of variables with current values. These allow the programmer to monitor the behaviour of individual variables and help prevent errors and unexpected side-effects.

Break points:
Points in the program where execution will pause. This helps the programmer to identify the position of errors.

(e) (i) 128 * 0.05 = 6.4 seconds

(ii) 128 = 2^7, 8 comparisons.
8 * 0.05 = 0.4 seconds

(iii) A binary search requires the file to be sorted.

31. (a) Any reasonable description of a section of pre-written code available for use by programmers.

(b)
```
set sum = 0
FOR digit = 1 TO 10
sum = sum + scanned(digit)
NEXT digit
set checksum = REMAINDER(sum,9)
IF checksum = scanned(maxarray) THEN
report VALID
ELSE prompt for rescan
```

(c) Any reasonable description of the use of a utility for line-by-line scanning of code for logic, or runtime, errors by programmer
More detail should be given regarding the reporting of variable values etc.

(d) (i) Examples of two difficulties are:
deletion from only one array results in wrong calculation of product numbers
sorting of arrays must be in parallel if numbers are to remain associated with correct items
any other valid point

(ii) Two alternatives might be 2D array or records
Note: Advantage should be clearly expressed

Section III – Part D Multimedia Technology

32. (a) (i) icon-based – use of preprogrammed buttons, icons or menus
script-based – input from keyboard to create commands

(ii) Icon-based – no commands need to be remembered, easier to create presentations using graphical images etc.
Script-based – more flexibility as user is not restricted to pre-given tools

(b) (i) MPC standards describe the minimum hardware specification requirements that a computer must have in order to be classified as a multimedia machine.

(ii) Any from:
64+Mb RAM, 333+MHz processor, backing storage (CD-R, CD-RW, Hard Disc), CD-ROMs (600kps), sound card (16-bit, MIDI playback), video (640x480x64).

(c) (i) Hypertext system allows the navigation of text using links – fundamental feature of WWW.

(ii) Compression reduces file size which reduces download time (and storage space).

(iii) Description of copyright laws as relevant to copying elements.

33. (a) Any three from:
Scaling – the image can be pulled or squeezed
Filling – using solid colours or patterns to fill in a shape
Clipping/Cropping – taking out unimportant detail from image
Morphing – joining two images together showing the transformation from one to the other
Smearing – rubbing over to produce a smudging effect
Blending – to mix different colours together
Gamma correction – changes brightness and ratios of colours.

33. (b)(i) JPEG, GIF, TIFF, BMP

(ii) JPEG – millions of colours can be used, common format, small size due to compression.
GIF – common format, lossless compression so original file stored as small file size.
TIFF – any number of colours and options available
BMP – Windows standard, uncompressed

(c) (i) CD-R or CD-RW (CD-ROM or CD not ascceptable) – common backing storage device can be used by clients, can store up to 850 Mb, durable, cheap and lightweight, portable
DVD-R (not DVD) – large storage up to 20Gb, faster access than CD

(ii) Wrong OS, not enough RAM, files saved in wrong format, no appropriate software on client's machine

34. (a) (i) Camera (or video digitiser) connected to computer via video capture card
Analogue to digital conversion required
Compression (MPEG) must be used before the frames can be saved

(ii) No analogue to digital conversion required, quality improved, faster to capture.

(b) (i) Fewer frames – less storage required but jerky motion.

(ii) More frames – smoother motion but more storage required.

(c) (i) Any two from:
Clips can be cropped
Frames can be deleted
Timeline can be used to change frames around
Transitions can be used to make video more interesting (fade in/out, dissolve, ripple etc)
Sound can be edited, removed or created

(ii) RAM – 128Mb + so that the clips can be viewed
Backing storage – 20Gb+ (video projects are large files even under compression)
Processor – 500MHz+ to ensure computer can cope with large projects with many frames.

35. (a) Lossy compression leads to a loss of information whereas lossless compression encodes data so that the original file can be recreated in its entirety.

(b) Text document is scanned to produce a bit map
A group of pixels are pattern matched against character (bit maps) stored within the OCR software
When a match is found the character's ASCII code is stored in a text output file

35. (c) ASCII (Plain text) – each character is stored but no formatting information is stored.
RTF (Rich Text Format) – formatting information (text font, size, style etc) is stored as well as the text itself.

(d) (i) Sampled – naturally occurring sounds
Synthesised – computer-generated sounds

(ii) Any two from:
Recording of sound into digitized data for future use
Playback of digitized sound
Allows connection of microphone, speakers, MIDI equipment
FM Synthesis where digitized sounds are generated mimicking natural sounds.

Computing Higher
2004

Section I

1. (a) They are stored (as lists of objects) where each object is represented by its attributes (or parameters or similar).

   (b) Rectangle, start co-ord, end co-ord, line thickness and fill colour.

2. (a) Any two from:
   - Address and data bus lines are used in parallel to represent binary numbers
   - Control bus lines are independent (discrete) of each other (different functions)
   - Address and Data buses carry data - Control Bus doesn't

   (b) 16 777 216 OR 2^{24} addresses

3. Any two from:
   - Type of interface eg serial, parallel, USB etc affects speed of transfer of data
   - Time taken to render single page in printer's memory
   - Size of buffer
   - Colour vs. b/w
   - Resolution of printer (not document)
   - Processor speed

4. Any two from:
   - Compensate for speed differences (data storage)
   - Compensate for differences in data format (data conversion) eg voltage, A to D, serial to parallel etc
   - Send control signals to peripheral
   - Device selection
   - Store status information

5. (i) The precision (or accuracy) is increased.
   (ii) The range of numbers which can be represented is increased.

6. (a) Transfer individual bytes (data/blocks of data) from storage device to processor.

   (b) Any one from:
   - Check that there is enough free memory for file
   - Allocate memory
   - Protect other processes
   - Keep track of free memory

7. (a) Description of any one from:
   - Parity check - check for even or odd no of 1s
   - Setting access rights - r,w,rw etc to prevent accidental change
   - Locking files at record level on a network so that only one user can make changes at one time.
   - Description of checksum

7. (b) Any one from:
   - Slower network performance due to extra bits being sent (eg parity, checksum)
   - Locking of records when another user is accessing them slows down access.
   - Extra processing required may slow down system

8. (a) One which can be accessed anywhere in the program.

   (b) array

9. (a) (i) Normal (in range), Extreme (boundary), Exceptional (out of range)
   (ii) **Normal** – e.g. 11 to 18 inclusive
   Extreme – e.g. 11,18
   Exceptional – e.g. 4, 25

   (b) Counting occurrences

10. Any two from:
    - Internal commentary
    - Meaningful identifiers
    - Embolden keywords
    - Blank lines
    - Indentation

11. (a) Any two from:
    - Interviewing clients
    - Observing workplace and making observation notes
    - Researching company information.

    (b) Any one from:
    - To describe how the problem will be solved.
    - To produce an algorithm.

    (c) Description of any one from:
    - **Pseudocode** - textual method showing operations and control structures in an algorithm.
    - **Structure diagram/chart** - graphical method showing structure of the program.
    - **Flowchart** - graphical method showing sequence and control structures.

12. (a) A mechanism (variable, data structure etc) for transferring data from one module to another (or the main program).

    (b) A pointer/reference to the value rather than the value itself is passed. When the value needs to be accessed/changed in the module, the reference is followed to the actual data.

13. Any two from:
    - Modules are already tested/error free
    - Modules are already written/documented
    - Don't have to type all the code
    - No time spent designing module

Section II

14. (a) Finding minimum

(b) (i) Any one from:
- To check for logic errors
- Make sure design meets specification
- Errors carried forward are expensive to correct.
- Not enough to say 'to check it is right'.

(ii) Work through algorithm on paper step by step using test data.

(c) **Error tracing tool:** One of:
- Inspecting/watching contents of variables (to help identify logic errors)
- Setting breakpoints in order to check values of variables at certain points (to help identify logic errors)
- Allows programmer to step through code (to determine location of logic errors)

Error reporting tool: to communicate location of errors, possibly give indication of error type

(d) One possible solution is:
```
CASE total of
     >750 : discount = 0.15
     501 to 750 : discount = 0.1
     251 to 500 : discount = 0.05
Otherwise
     Discount = 0
Discounted bill = bill * (1 - discount)
```
Multiple or nested If statements are also acceptable if correct.

(e) (i) An internationally agreed data format which many applications are written to accept.

(ii) One from:
- Departments may not all have the same software (or same versions of software)
- Data saved using standards can be input into most software they might be using

15. (a) (i) One hardware and one software from:
- Network interface cards
- Network card
- Wireless network card
- Network OS
- Communication software

(ii) Bus, star, ring are acceptable here, not mesh.
Star:

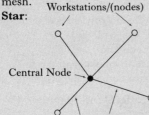

Workstations/(nodes)

Central Node

Channel/cables/wires/ communication link/wireless

15. (b) Any two from:
- Install faster processors in their machines to improve response times (or faster server)
- Install more RAM to hold more data
- Upgrade (or add) specialised graphics card with reason
- Faster network card with reason
- New motherboard (with good reason)
- Higher bandwidth cabling with reason

(c) (i) Virus protection software to reduce likelihood of attacks from viruses attached to files, compression utilities (eg winzip), download manager/accelerator to increase speed, firewall (must give reason in each case)

(ii) Disc clean up program to remove temporary files left by accessing pages, de-fragmentation program to optimise free space on the hard drive to save downloaded file.

(d) Any two from:
- No pre-determined order of activity
- Actions attached to clicking of objects to increase interactivity
- Pre-defined code for buttons, dialog boxes, etc which allows easy creation of a GUI

16. (a) (i) By value as the parameters are not being changed.

(ii) Accept (or similar) – string OR char OR boolean

(b) One possible solution is:
```
set control variable to false
repeat
    ask user for licence details
    if(licence<>'Y' AND licence <>'N') then
        display error message
    else
        set control variable to true
    end if
until control variable = true
```

(c) One possible solution is:
```
If drive='Y' and Age='Y' and Years='Y' then
    Accept='Y'
Else
    Accept='N'
Endif
```

(d) Company may change OS, peripherals, upgrade computers.

(e) Any one from:
- **Procedural** - Program follows step by step algorithm, necessary data types, operators etc can be supported by language.
- **Declarative** – Problem can be defined in terms of facts + rules, rules can be applied to inputs to give interview Y or N response, queries can be pattern matched to give solutions, searching built in etc.

Computing Higher
2004 (cont.)

17. (a) (i) One from:
- Problem/requirements specification
- System specification

(ii) Descriptions of any two from:
- meaningful error messages
- consistent commands
- minimum user input
- help facilities
- ability for user to reverse actions
- simple actions
- take into account users' experience etc

(b) (i) Program which has been broken down into smaller problems/tasks which are handled in procedures/functions

(ii) Parameter passing, using procedures, use of local variables, use of libraries

(c) **Software House** - to fully test and make sure the program is working efficiently and correctly **Insurance Company** - to ensure program can work with its end users and to highlight any possible errors or concerns not picked up by the Software House. May provide test data.

(d) Any two from:
- Large amount of RAM depending on number of clients involved (number of records)
- Fast processor speed to process records and carry out calculations in acceptable time.
- Peripherals involved etc **but must link back to the problem**

18. (a) **Database**:
- No (or less) coding required
- System can be created relatively quickly.
- Database program has already been tested for errors.

OR

New program:
- Can be written to their precise specifications. (Custom features)
- File formats can be optimised to make best use of backing storage.
- Custom HCI can be created.

(b) 2400 x 800 = 1920000 pixels
16 bits/pixel => 2 × 1920000 = 3840000 bytes
3840000/1024 = 3750 kilobytes
3750/1024 = **3·66 megabytes**

(c) Hard Disk, DVD-Writer - Approximately 1600 Mb of storage required

(d) (i) Some possible answers are:
- To allow hierarchical access to network to differentiate between levels of staff based on user name etc.
- Password protect database file and only give password to security.
- Use encryption to prevent unauthorised access to files.
- Physical protection.

18. (d)(ii) For example, for **encryption**: even if file is copied from hard drive it will still not be accessible unless the decryption key is known.

(e) Any two from:
- **Modular programming** - Program consists of procedures which carry out specific functions. This makes it easier to identify areas which may require changes to be made.
- **Internal commentary** - Comments inserted into code to give information about purpose of that piece of code. Again identifies areas which may need to be changed.
- **Parameter passing** - Any external data required by a module is passed in through parameters making modules self contained. This may allow machine specific modules to be replaced by equivalent ones written for target system.
- Use of **meaningful identifiers** make program more readable
- **Non processor specific** code

19. (a) Any one from:
- Sounds may be used to alert partially-sighted users to particular actions
- Sounds may provide an audible alert to busy users instead of using a dialog box

(b) (i) Signed bit: 11111000
Two's complement: 10001000

(ii) Any two from:
- Signed bit does not support binary addition rules.
- Signed bit has two values for zero (or two zeros positive and negative).
- Two's complement is "symmetric" around zero.

(c) 1. Set up the address bus with the address of the next instruction to be fetched.
2. Activate read line on the control bus.
3. Instruction fetched along the data bus.
4. Decode and execute the instruction.

(d) (i) Any one from:
- Different machine code/instruction set/object code.
- Different word size/bus widths/control lines.
- Different processor architecture/number of registers.

(ii) Any one from:
- Use an emulator program.
- Cross compile the original source code.

Section III - Artificial Intelligence
20. (a) (i) X = yellow
(ii) 4

20. (b) Process involves these 6 steps:
1. Match at line 22 with carnivore(grinder). First sub-goal is eats(grinder Y)
2. Match at line 20 Y is "grass"
3. Second sub-goal of line 22 is now not(plant(grass))
4. Goal plant(grass) fails
5. Not (plant(grass)) is true
6. Therefore carnivore(grinder) is **true**

(c) (i) A "grinder" eats grass so is clearly a herbivore.
(ii) The plant "grass" is not in the knowledge base.

(d) no / fail / false

(e) cannibal(X) IF beetle(X _) AND eats (X Y) AND beetle(Y _).

21. (a) **Knowledge Base** - list of facts and rules known to the system
Inference Engine – compares query with facts and rules to find solution
Explanatory/User Interface – interprets the commands of the user and relays results

(b) **Advantage** - any one from:
- No need to code interface or inference engine
- Lower programming skill required
- Faster implementation as don't need to form Prolog type queries

Disadvantage: can be restrictive and inflexible (give justification)

(c) (i) Explanation of assigning a numerical value to probability (0 to 1, 0 to 100% etc). Valid example (which need not correspond to any given syntax) such as:

```
if symptom(XXX) then error(YYY, 0.1 )
```

(ii) One of:
- Description of the suggestion of a number of results (with degree of likelihood) as providing a better diagnostic tool in the search for solution to an unknown problem
- Increase user confidence in the system.

(d) **Why:** Why is the current question being asked?
How: How was the advice/conclusion reached?

22. (a) Any two from:
- Size of memory (RAM) restricted the size of the active search space
- Small/expensive backing storage limited the size of knowledge base held
- Slower/less complex processor increased run time needed
- Other valid description

(b) (i)

Depth First   Breadth First

22. (b) (ii) **Depth First** – since it only holds the current search path and is thus more memory efficient.

(c) One from:
- Restricts the size of the search space.
- Predicts where the goal is most likely to be thus reducing time taken.

(d) Any two from:
- Make the rule base dynamic (let it learn new rules and/or adapt old ones).
- Increase the amount of RAM to hold all possible states.
- Use a neural net to learn the best strategies.
- Use heuristics to narrow search space (not heuristics on own).

(e) Descriptions of any two from:
- Background noise may obscure voice input.
- User's voice may change because of illness, accent etc.
- Too large a vocabulary for the game.
- Digitising sound and pattern matching with stored commands may take too long.
- Similar sounding words, to, too etc.

23. (a) Any two from:
- Software is less liable to corruption.
- ROM is more physically robust compared to magnetic disk.
- Load time is quicker.

(b) (i) Any two from:
- distance perception to allow navigation of obstacles
- depth perception to allow objects to be picked up
- wrongful interpretation of shadows/colour variations as bogus edges of objects

(ii) For example, use of two cameras to provide binocular vision in first two bullet points. Accept slightly vague answers about use of lights & high resolution cameras to give better information to processing software if they are explicitly tied into reason in part (i).

(c) (i) A system which is modelled on the structure of the human brain. Consists of artificial neurons with several inputs and one output. The output connects to another artificial neuron The output fires if the combined inputs exceed a certain value (threshold).

(ii) Each input has a weighting. Weightings are adjusted until correct output is achieved.

(d) Examples of acceptable responses are:
- **Pro** – machines cannot make independent decisions about situations that they have not been programmed to deal with
- **Con** – intelligence can be defined in terms of performing reasonable independent actions in the absence of hard facts, machines can be capable of learning (or recognising images, handwriting etc)

Computing Higher
2004 (cont.)

Section III - Computer Networking

24. (*a*) (i) Retransmits data because the limit of distance has been exceeded. Need idea of boosting signal.

    (ii) Physical layer

    (iii) Both companies use the same protocol.

(*b*) Any two from:
- **Proxy server** – allows caching, network address translation etc.
- **Email** – receives, stores and transmits email
- **Print** - allows station to use a printer not connected to it.

(*c*) **Advantages**
- Do daily backups of the fileserver,
- Installation/upgrade of software can be controlled.
- Access to files can be centrally controlled.
- Security controlled more easily.

Disadvantages
- Failure of the server
- More expensive for servers
- Network congestion

(*d*) Use a firewall to filter access

(*e*) TCP splits data into packets and adds header to each one. IP adds its own header to allow the packet to be routed around the intranet.

25. (*a*) Descriptions of any two from:
- Higher bandwidth cabling
- Adoption of standard protocols
- Improvement in wireless technology
- Improvements in communications software
- Faster/cable modems

(*b*) (i) Amount of data that can be transmitted in a given time by a network connection

    (ii) **Data compression** – decreasing the size of a file, possibly by removing redundant, repeated data prior to transmission, once received it is enlarged again.

    Caching – storing components of web pages on the local hard drive and retrieving from there when the pages are accessed again.

(*c*) Descriptions of any two from:
- DON'T USE UPPER CASE – it's shouting
- No flaming
- Don't send chain letters.
- If you are forwarding don't change original.
- Allow time for mail to be received and read – time differences between nations.

(*d*) Access rights can be used to control a user's level of permission to view/change a file.

25. (*e*) **Application** – top layer which provides a set of interfaces for applications to obtain access to networked services.

Transport – maintains connection between communicating systems ensuring integrity of data using error detection and correction, ensures data is error free and sent in right order/sequence.

26. (*a*) **Fibre Optic**:
- Faster communication speed (higher bandwidth)
- More secure
- Fewer transmission errors
- No electrical interference so fewer transmission errors

Twisted Pair:
- Cheaper
- Easier to extend network

(*b*) **Advantage**
- easier to extend
- failure of one cable only affects one node
- less collisions in a star

Disadvantage
- additional hardware needed
- failure of central node would cause network to fail

(*c*) **Carrier sense/multiple access** – any station that detects traffic won't transmit

Collision detect – upon detecting collision waits a random time to transmit again

(*d*) $5 \cdot 5 \times 1024 \times 1024 \times 8/100\,000\,000$ = **0.46 secs**

(*e*) Any two from:
- Data integrity – such as parity bits, checksum
- Not all of the bandwidth available to one user
- Collisions involving resending
- Errors in transmission requires retransmission

27. (*a*) Descriptions of any two from:
- Reach a wider customer base.
- Access to Internet resources such as up-to-date info from other sites.
- Ability to email customers and organisations.
- Working outside office – with valid reason

(*b*) **ADSL** OR **ISDN** OR **Cable** – always on, known cost, higher bandwidth, continued access to voice calls etc.

(*c*) **Encryption** – description of encoding when sending and decoding when received

(*d*) Any one from e-mail, and any one from file transfer:

E-mail
- **POP3** - is used for receiving e-mail
- **SMTP** - is used for sending e-mail across the internet

File transfer
- **FTP** - is used to transfer files between two computers
- **HTTP** - used for transferring web pages.

27. (e) **For:** Since better off people have access to computer equipment they will access cheaper products (not available in High Street) and so widen gap.

Against: Companies will save money and pass cheaper costs onto all consumers so poor will benefit too.

28. (a) 1. Top of stack is located.
   2. Item copied to memory.
   3. Pointer to top of stack is decremented by one.

(b) Error message needs to be generated with alternate action (error trapping). (if stack pointer = 0 then error message)

(c)

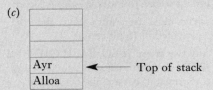

Top of stack

(d) (i) Any two of:
   • Bubble sort
   • Quicksort
   • Insertion sort
   • Selection sort

(ii) **Memory efficiency**
   • *Bubble* – List memory +1 location
   • *Quick* – List memory +1 location
   • *Insertion* – List memory +1 location
   • *Selection* – Double size of list

Processor efficiency
   • *Bubble* – Max of n(n-1)/2 comparisons made
   • *Quick* – Of order n log n
   • *Insertion* – Max of n(n-1)/2 comparisons
   • *Selection* – Max of n(n-1) comparisons

29. (a) (i) **Two dimensional array**: data structure consisting of multiple storage locations - each location indexed by two numbers.

(ii) **Record**: elements may be of different types, components referenced by name rather than position.

(b) (i) No built in link between parallel arrays so sort may become unsynchronised. All data in record moved together.

(ii) Once data found in one array, data from corresponding position in parallel array extracted. Searching would identify record and so all data retrieved.

(c) Example: A list of forenames and surnames have to be stored so that they can be sorted on surname. The reason for using two dimensional arrays is that both data items are of the same type.

(d) **Interpreter**: loop translated for each pass.
Compiler: loop initially translated and then run from object code.

30. (a) New items are added at the rear of the queue and items are removed from the front of the queue. The item being removed has been the longest in the queue and hence FIFO (First In First Out).

(b) (i)

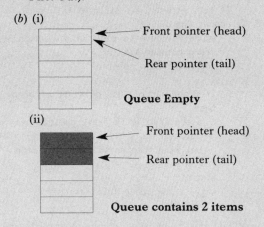

Queue Empty

(ii)

Queue contains 2 items

(c) One of three possible answers, depending on how the queue is implemented:
   1. Wrap around takes place and the new item is added to the start of the array where an item has been removed:

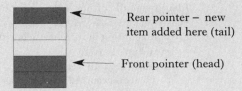

Rear pointer – new item added here (tail)

Front pointer (head)

OR

   2. As the queue empties from the front the items in the queue move forward into the empty array elements so the new item will be added to the end of the queue:

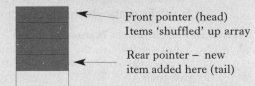

Front pointer (head) Items 'shuffled' up array

Rear pointer – new item added here (tail)

OR

   3. A 'queue full' message will be given and the new element 'lost':

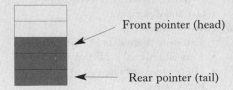

Front pointer (head)

Rear pointer (tail)

Computing Higher
2004 (cont.)

30. (d) One possible answer is:

```
If rear pointer + 1 still within array
bounds then
    store key code in position indicated by¬
        rear pointer + 1
    increment rear pointer
else
    if front pointer not at start of array
    then
        store keycode in first position in¬
            array
        set rear pointer to first position
    end if
else
    write error queue full message
    end if
```

31. (a) Data must be in order, all data must be directly accessible ie resident in memory or stored in direct access backing store.

(b) 1. Identify Joe and Pete's as middle of list
2. Compare Farmhouse Feasts to Joe and Pete's and so discard lower section of list
3. Identify middle of new list as Farmhouse Feasts

(c) (i) Possible counting occurrences algorithm:

```
Initialise counter
For each item in the list
    if item=required recipe then add¬
        one to counter
    Next item
Report value of counter
```

(ii) One array would store names of all main courses offered and the second would store the corresponding number of times chosen. Search for course chosen in first array.

Section III – Multimedia Technology

32. (a) (i) Video which allows the user to choose options and navigate through the video.
(ii) One from:
- It allows users to follow different paths through the multimedia presentation.
- Can answer questions and receive feedback

(b) (i) CD-ROM, CD-R, CD-RW, audio CD, CD-I and description
(ii) Any two from:
- Can store more data (4.7Gb to 17Gb)
- Less vibrational problems with drives
- Higher transfer rate (up to 9Mbps 2 times faster)

(c) (i) Faster download, smaller file sizes, useful for WAP
(ii) Any two from:
- Easy to get lost or disorientated within the system.
- Too much information at the one time
- Difficult to pinpoint topic area due to large volume of choices
- May encounter broken links

32. (d) Descriptions of any two from:
- Video/graphics cards to enable capturing, editing and storage of video frames
- Improved sound cards to enable input, DAC, ADC and output of sound
- High capacity RAM to allow viewing of media elements
- Fast processors to allow fast capture and downloading
- High resolution, large, colour monitors to view media elements

33. (a) (i) **Resolution** - How many pixels per inch is used
Bit Depth - How many colours per pixel are in the image
(ii) Final file size (for storage etc) is lower

(b) The image must use fewer colours than the range provided in 16 bit colour

(c) (i) Any two from: JPEG, TIFF, GIF, BMP
(ii) **JPEG** – loss of quality due to lossy compression, large range of colours
GIF – restricted to 256 colours, lossless compression
TIFF – quality not lost, no compression, cross platform
BMP – quality not lost, no compression, Windows standard

(d) Descriptions of any two from:
- Takes too long to load (eg too many frames used for the animation)
- Monitor may not be correctly set up (eg wrong resolution, bit depth, refresh rate)
- Correct software may not be on the computer system

34. (a) (i) Standard buttons can be used, easy to position objects, no start or end point in programming code.
(ii) More flexibility in code, not tied to buttons and other objects set in an icon based system.

(b) **Hardware** may not be capable of handling the data rate.
Software may not be optimised for recording – virtual memory may not be switched off, full colour setting for monitor may not be set, etc.

(c) (i) High storage requirements due to frame rate. Compression required to create smaller files.
(ii) **MPEG** (Motion Picture Expert Group) – High compression using lossy techniques
Quicktime – Mac standard
AVI (Audio Video Interleave) – Windows standard which can use various compression techniques such as Indeo, MSVC, RLE.

34. (*d*) **Input** – Video camera (to record frames) and video capture card (to capture onto computer system) (conversion from analogue to digital if analogue camera). Alternative answers using digital video and firewire port acceptable.

Process – Video editing software to edit the frames, or insert clip using authoring software, or compression.

Output – Video card (for decompression, possible VRAM) and high resolution monitor for viewing.

35. (*a*) Video/animation to show tutorials, voice playback of help facilities, animated icons (e.g. expanding trash)

(*b*) Descriptions of any one from:
- **CMF** (Creative Music Format) – uses instruments defined in a file
- **ROL** – similar to CMF but uses a different instruments' file
- **MOD** – uses digitised instruments played at different sampling frequencies
- **WAV** – Window standard, simple sound file with a short file header
- **MP3** – uses compression to compact files
- **MIDI** – most commonly used format – need description
- **AIFF** – Audio Interchange File Format with description

(*c*) (i) Digitising the voice, ADC, sound file compression (setting bit depth and sample rate)

(ii) Any two from:
- **Fade in/out** – gradually increasing/decreasing the volume
- **Cross fade** – allows 2 audio clips to be joined together smoothly
- **Echo** – to provide effect of a large area/space
- **Panning** – toggling between left and right channels
- **Combining** – adding to audio clip
- **Transpose** – changing the sampling rate
- **Looping** – repeating a sample
- **Cropping** – removing unwanted sections

(iii) Ensure adequate sample rate, ensure quality of sound system is high enough, eliminate background noise.

Computing Higher 2005
Old Arrangements

Section I

1. Extra software running, processor time, extra bits onto transmitted data.

2. (*a*) Area of memory (RAM)

(*b*) Used to temporarily store data in transit between CPU and printer
or
Holding document while CPU is processing other tasks.

3. (i) exponent.

(ii) mantissa.

4. (i) Each object/graphic is stored as a list of instructions/attributes/parameters.

(ii) Start x, start y, line width, line colour, fill colour etc.

5. Any two from:
- Ability to include pre-defined menus, buttons, windows etc.
- Program consists of blocks of code attached to events (event handlers).
- No pre-defined route through program.

6. Any two from: virus checker, defragger, disk formatter, compression program, file recovery, cloning (imaging) software (note: no commercial names like WINZIP).

7. txt, rtf, ASCII.

8. Any two from:
- To automate a complex sequence of operations/speed up productivity.
- To customise/extend the functionality of the application.

9. Any two from: print, file, internet, multimedia (CD), mail, proxy, application etc.

10. Any two from:
- Larger programs can be loaded at once (no need for virtual memory).
- Fewer fetches required to backing storage.
- Good description of using Cache RAM.

11. • Document detailing the exact problem which the client would like a solution to
- Legal binding contract between parties
- Details of the task that the system will perform.

Computing Higher 2005
Old Arrangements (cont.)

12. Any two from:

Interview – question employees on current methods.

Observation – go into work place and study current practice, taking notes.

Study documentation – examine input and output which is required.

Questionnaire – generate information from many employees by issuing questionnaire.

13. Adaptive: the actual function of the software does not need to be changed, it just needs to be altered to accept input from a different source.

14. Any two from:
* Top down (or stepwise refinement): start with problem and break it into sub-problems,
  – break these smaller problems into smaller problems, repeat until you have manageable problems to solve.
* Bottom up: other way round.
* Pseudocode: written design uses english terms, language independent.
* Flowchart: graphical representation which shows dataflow.
* Structure chart: graphical representation which shows structure and dataflow.

15. Any two from:

Design HCI – screen layouts, user prompts, help information.
* design of test data
* produce algorithm of solution / plan events or objects and operations
* in depth structured walkthrough explanation.

16. It does not meet the original problem as defined in the requirements/software/problem/specification/operational requirements.

17. Global variable

18. (*a*) • normal: 7, 8, 9 – test with data that should be accepted
* extreme/boundary/limits: 6, 10 – test the boundaries of what is accepted
* exceptional/invalid: 15, -3, f – test that incorrect data is not accepted

(*b*) age < 6 OR age > 10
age >= 6 AND age <=10
age>5 AND age <11

(*c*) String array, array of strings

Section II

19. (*a*) Any two from:
* can divide it between them and work on a bit each
* break problem into smaller, more manageable parts
* can test modules separately first, before joining together
* can use parameter passing
* use of module library
* improves readability

(*b*) Any two from:

Editor: to enter and amend code

Translator: to turn the program into machine code, to run it

Error tracing tool / Debugger: to find errors in code

Error Reporter: reporting back errors with type or location

(*c*) Any two from:

Documentation for the program: user guide to explain how to operate (install) the software

Technical guide to explain requirements to run program

Tutorial Guide to teach how to use software

Software license – legal requirement if software is copyrighted

(*d*) Highlight commands – e.g. capitals, colour

Description of white space – e.g. indentation, spacing to show structure of program

Modular code – splitting code into sections

(*e*) Syntax error, e.g. PIRNT "Hello"

Logic error, e.g. area = length+breadth

Run time error, e.g. division by zero

Linking error, e.g. library method used by program missing

20. (*a*) Bitmapped – allows individual pixels to be edited

or

All digital photographs are bitmapped.

(*b*) $4 \times 6 \times 800 \times 800 \times 16$ bits = 245760000 bits
/ 8 = bytes
/ 1024 = kb
/ 1024 = 29·3 Mb

(*c*) (i) USB stick / Flash memory card, floppy disk, Zip disk, CD-R, CD-RW, DVD-R, DVD-RW

(ii) May be physical component of digital camera, therefore no need to write from camera to another medium. (Note: the choice must be appropriate for storing image files.)

20. (d) Resolution 1200dpi – high quality photographs required
Bit-depth 24 bit– real life (true) colour required in photographs
Print speed 12 ppm– fast to meet demand of many customers
Different paper sizes – customers may require varying sizes of photographs
Type of interface – speed of data transfer
Buffer – to store images

(e) (i) MIPS
FLOPS (MFlops)
A benchmark

(ii) MIPS – measures how many millions of instructions are processed in a second
FLOPS (MFLOPS) - measures how many floating point instructions are processed in a second
Benchmark – measures a certain criteria defined by the benchmark (numbers must be mentioned to quantify processor performance).

21. (a) (i) Any one from:
Actual client has an opportunity to ensure that software meets requirements
Bank can comment on program's operation

(ii) Any one from:
Comments made by client can allow changes to be made
Could prevent corrective maintenance later.

(b) (i) The program produces correct results every time it is run, not stopping due to design faults

(ii) Any two from:
Exhaustive testing – where all levels of test data is used with all levels of possible users
Each stage within the SDP is thoroughly checked and compared with requirements specification
Module Testing
Beta Testing (with description)

(c)
```
Max= hits (1)
For Page=2 to total number of pages do
  If hits(page) > max then
    Max= hits(page)
  Endif
End loop
```
or
```
Max= 0
For Page=1 to total number of pages do
  If hits(page) > max then
    Max= hits(page)
End loop
```

21. (d) Video, sound etc. may not be seen, heard, ensure appropriate plug-ins are installed, correct hardware (such as cards, speakers, monitors etc) are used.
Not enough RAM or processing power etc. to view pages, ensure computers have minimum specification for Internet access.
Downloading files linking to viruses, bandwidth, storage space, use filtering techniques.

22. (a) Does not crash and/or stop due to unexpected input

(b) (i) Parameter passed is the actual variable itself (or the address of same), any changes to the parameter persist beyond the call.

(ii) Current value of variable is passed in, any changes do not affect the original value.
A copy is made and this copy is used in the subprogram, the original is left unchanged.

(iii) Pass by value is preferable because if the variable needs to be used by other modules then its value will be unchanged on exit from subprogram.

(c)
```
set found to zero
for each item in list
if name$ = array(index) then
set found to index
next item
if found = 0 then display error
```

(d) IF unexplained > 0 OR (absence_total > 5 AND staff_query > 0) THEN Send_letter

23. (a) $2^{32} \times 24$ bits = 12Gb

(b) Any two of the following:
Data storage (buffering)
Data conversion/voltage differences
Device selection
Control information
Status information.

(c) Compiler or interpreter

(Choice must be clear)
Compiled code can be saved so that it does not need to be recompiled each time the game is run.
Game will not be held up while code is translated as with interpreted code.
Interpreter would be better for debugging at creation stage.

(d) Address bus is set up with the address to be written to
Data bus is set up with data to be written
Write line on control bus is activated.
Data is transferred from processor to memory

Computing Higher 2005
Old Arrangements (cont.)

24. (a) Undo
Dialogue boxes that prompt for confirmation of destructive actions (verification)
Locking (greying out) inappropriate options

(b) Event-driven
- predefined controls and routines (buttons, windows, library calls etc)
- range of data types
- range of control structures
- arithmetic functions
- etc.
or
Procedural
- library of routines
- range of data types
- range of control structures
- arithmetic functions
- etc.

(c) Protect other processes
Check there is enough free memory
Select the area of memory to place the process.

(d) Bit depth – the lower the value the more memory freed for other tasks.
– too low and certain data cannot successfully be represented.
Resolution – the lower the value the more memory freed for other tasks.

(e) Processing of background tasks would cause foreground tasks to slow down reducing system performance.

Section III – Artificial Intelligence

25. (a) (i) X=neptune
(ii) X= saturn   Y=titan
X=neptune   Y = nereid

(b) Goal satellite (titan B)
match at 10 Sub Goal orbits(titan B)
Match at 8 B= Saturn

Goal satellite (titan B)
Match at 11 Sub Goal orbits(titan Z)
Match at 8 Z= Saturn
Backtrack to 11 New Sub Goal satellite(saturn B)
Match at 10 New Sub Goal orbits(saturn B)
Match at 7 B=the_sun

Return solution B=the_sun

(c) moon_of(X,Y) if orbits (X, Y) and planet (Y)

(d) Knowledge base does not know that Neptune orbits the Sun
Knowledge base does not know that Nereid orbits the Sun

25. (e) Any one from:
Huge number of known stars
Large number of objects involved in orbiting the stars.
Difficulties in the definitions of objects.

26. (a) Domain expert

(b) Inference engine – does the reasoning/searching
User Interface – allows users to enter queries, outputs results of queries.

(c) **Backward chaining**
ADVISE finder IS legal owner
IF item IS reported found AND
crown IS not claiming.
or
Forward chaining
IF item IS reported found AND
crown IS not claiming
THEN ADVISE finder IS legal owner.

(d) Domain expert or lawyer will be involved in checking the output advice is correct.

(e) The user can be held responsible as the expert system is to be treated as reference like a book.

(f) Against – need to code the search methods
For – ability to create a friendly HCI using existing controls and built-in functions.

27. (a) Definitions of intelligence are not static but evolving, e.g. showing intelligent behaviour.
Many different aspects of intelligence.
Ambiguity of intelligence.

(b) Expert system –justification of *why* a question is asked and *how* advice is reached.
Neural network – cannot explain its reasoning as no algorithm is used.

(c) (i) Depth – goes down the first branch of nodes first until none is left in that path and then goes back up to the most recent branch
Breadth – all nodes are visited on a level before progressing to the next level.
(ii) Depth-first since only the current path need be stored.
(iii) Given several different starting paths from any given node – they could be evaluated independently.

28. (a) (i) Ability of a computer system to understand human language.
(ii) Expanding/evolving nature of human language/slang.
Ambiguity in meaning of sentences.
Same word can have different meanings etc.

(b) (i) Could search for phrases based on the same meaning so that searching on fever would not result in phrases such as 'patient didn't have fever'.

28. (b) (ii) Less likely to have to introduce new words as often as everyday language.
Words have clearly defined meanings (less ambiguity) and are unlikely to have two meanings.
Certain phrases will be in common usage among medical practitioners.

(c) Faster clock speeds, allowing searching of the database to be completed quickly.
More memory, allowing more data to be held for processing and allowing larger applications to be run.
Parallel processing, allowing more parsing tasks to be carried out simultaneously.

(d) Sort in descending order of Certainty Factors – Certainty Factors are numerical values measuring success of the match, e.g. 1 for most likely to 0 for least likely.

Section III - Computer Networking

29. (a) (i) client-server: server computer provides services/resources to other computers (clients) on the network.
peer-to-peer: every computer on the network has equal status and can pass messages/share files etc.

(ii) • game and associated files held on central server means data and game state are up-to-date.
• central control of access rights make game state more secure.
• dedicated game server may be faster in terms of access to shared files/software.

(b) (i) The domain name address is the address of the computer holding the file (www.WebGrafters.co.uk).

(ii) Resource name is the name of the file(s) to be downloaded (Spider.zip in the updates folder).

(c) (i) TCP breaks down file into packets
TCP adds header to each packet
IP adds IP address header to each packet
IP routes packet around network
TCP reassembles the packets

(ii) Name of a suitable protocol (HTTP, FTP).

(d) (i) $(112 \times 8)/15 = 59\cdot73$ seconds (or 1 minute)
(ii) • bad packets needing re-sent
• available bandwidth
• rest of message frame takes up space and hence bandwidth
• another part of the network between host and students may be slower connection etc.
• any other valid reason.

30. (a) (i) Bridge or router
(ii) Internetwork
(iii) Any one of the following:
• no telephone costs
• more reliable/secure
• faster access/download time
• any other valid answer.

(b) (i) Any valid server: (communication/web/mail, print, CD)
(ii) Any two valid methods other than access rights or passwords (e.g. encryption, firewall).

(c) Checks if line is free if so station will transmit when there is no network traffic.
If line is busy all transmitting stations stop transmitting if multiple signals detected and will wait a random time before retransmitting.

(d) Fibre optic cable (ISDN)– high bandwidth and can't be tapped in to.
or Signal does not deteriorate with distance so no repeaters required.

31. (a) (i) Meeting costs (travel etc), time savings
(ii) Web cam, TV/screen, microphone, speakers, modem.

(b) (i) • Repeater operates at the Physical layer
• Bridge operates at the Data link layer
• Router operates at the Network layer.
(ii) • Physical - addresses physical characteristics of the network, e.g. cabling, connectors etc (electrical/mechanical characteristics).
• Data link - addresses size of packet, means of addressing packet, preventing two nodes transmitting at same time (link, error and flow control).
• Network - routes packets from one network to another (routing, switching and flow control over a network).
• Presentation – formats and encrypts data that is sent across the network.
• Application – supports user applications across the network.
• Transport – responsible for transport of data between systems.
• Session – Establishes, manages and terminates connections between application in a network.

(c) • Ensure compatibility of hardware and software around world.
• Allow hardware and software from different manufacturers to be interconnected.
• etc.

(d) (i) Each device has a unique identifier to prevent addressing errors
(ii) 48 bit address => 2^{48}.

Computing Higher 2005

Old Arrangements (cont.)

32. (a) • faster or more reliable network cabling or other hardware (switches etc)
    • better networking software, easier to install and/or configure
    • greater standardization of hardware/software through protocols or data standards
    • any other acceptable answer.

    (b) (i) One mark for description of star, bus, ring or tree. Diagram accepted, but must have correct name and at least two labels.
        (ii) For example for 'star' – reduce congestion when using high bandwidth resources such as video clips.

    (c) (i) Data loss through corruption, etc.
        (ii) Valid strategy involving regular backups taken and held elsewhere.
        Raider or Mirror Server with explanation.

    (d) (i) Circuit-switching is where a circuit is established between sender and receiver prior to transmission and is maintained throughout transmission. (leased lines etc)
        (ii) Independent routing of packets in packet-switching makes networks more flexible and robust. Also the lack of need for extra hardware/software makes this method cheaper.
        (iii) The actual transfer is faster as there is no addressing information transmitted, also packets do not need to be re-assembled by the receiver.

Section III – Computer Programming

33. (a) Edit text, copy and paste, move, delete etc.

    (b) (i) Looping too many times unnecessarily. Condition not being met so loop continues regardless.
        (ii) Looping too many times or infinitely is a waste of memory and processing time.

    (c) (i) The list must be put into numerical order.
        (ii) set top to top of list
        set bottom to bottom of list
        repeat
            calculate middle as (top + bottom)/2
            If this value at middle is less than the search item then
                set bottom to middle+1
            else
                set top to middle-1
            end if
        until search item found or bottom > top

    (d) When the item is near the beginning of a large list.

34. (a) A construct which allows many items of data to be constructed as a single set.

    (b) (i) Different data types are required **or** 4 different items of data are used.
        (ii) A record could be used or linked lists
        Record candidate;
        Name: string
        Number: integer
        Subject: string
        Pass: character

    (c) Create file, open file, append file, close file, read from file + justification related to problem.

    (d) Counting occurrences.

    (e) Bubble, selection, selection exchange + description.

35. (a) (i) To detect, locate and correct errors.
        (ii) Dry run – to use a structured listing to manually go through a code's logic.
        Step by step execution – to locate position of error.
        Watch window (or similar) – to follow the values of variables as the program is running.
        Breakpoints – stopping the program at key points as it is running.

    (b) 1 d array of string.

    (c) Ask user for fruit to be found (search_fruit)
        Set position to 1
        Set occurrences to 0
        Repeat
            If fruit(position)= search_fruit then
                Increment occurrence by 1
            Increment position by 1
        Until end of list

    (d) (i) Different data types are used.
        (ii) The pointer found for the position to be inserted must correspond to the name array and quantity array. The position of fruits and quantities below must then be incremented by 1.

36. (a) (i) Stack – LIFO. Data item last to be added to the list is the first to be dealt with
        Queue – FIFO Data item first to be added to the list is the first to be dealt with.
        (ii) Head (start), tail (end).

    (b) (i) Geography is put in position 1
        End pointer points at position 1
        (ii) Geography is put in position 2
        End pointer moves to position 2

    (c) let top = top – 1
        let stack (top) = subject

    (d) stack
        current state is pushed onto stack
        when interrupt is complete pop stack and continue

Section III – Multimedia Technology

37. (a) Record the comments into his computer using microphone with sound card.
Analogue to digital conversion.
Import the clip into the presentation using the presentation software.

(b) As MM developed not all current computers had the hardware to play the multimedia.
The MPC standard meant that buyers would know that their computer had minimum performance standards.

(c) (i) Use 'change brightness' to improve the colour of the photo
Use colour palette to improve colour
Use bit-map editing tool to colour pixels affected by tear in original photograph.
Blending – combining pixels based on tonal or colour value.

(ii) Any two from:
Improve size and resolution of video window, e.g. for better quality video
Improve hard drive size e.g. to accommodate larger software.
Increase RAM, e.g. to aid smooth video editing
Increase CD ROM speed, e.g. to make faster access and smoother playback
Interfaces for faster data transfer rates, buffering etc.

(d) More precision, e.g. in timings within presentation
More flexibility in creation of presentation

38. (a) Any two from:
Links between screens, e.g. timings, transitions
Content of screens, e.g. placement of items, actual content
Common features, e.g. backgrounds, style sheets
Navigation links.

(b) Any two from:
Try all links to make sure they function as specified
Play all videos, sound and animations
Ask 'typical users' to beta test it.

(c) Each frame created using graphics software.
Frames then played back in sequence.

(d) (i) Any one from:
Files are large and take up a lot of backing storage; compression reduces the amount of backing storage needed.

(ii) Any one from:
Reduce frame rate, reduce bit-depth, resolution, reduction in frame size.

(e) (i) Detail in the video may be removed by the compression technique used.
Decompression takes time so playback may be affected.

(ii) Use a lossless compression technique which preserves all the original information.

39. (a) 16 bit quality now gives CD quality audio
Ability to store waveform tables to simulate instruments
MIDI interface available
Can mix or combine sounds
Increased number of channels
Increased on board RAM
Increased on board processor (DSP).

(b) Both have dedicated coprocessors to relieve main processor
Provide additional RAM
Analogue to digital conversion.

(c) Identify 'cough' section of wave by playing audio and noting positions.
Crop/delete unwanted sections of wave.

(d) Any two from:
Reduce from stereo to mono (1 track instead of two)
Half the samples recorded (sample rate reduced)
Half the number of bits used (sample size/resolution reduced).

(e) Playing high quality sound 'slows a computer down' so their work in the application may be a little sluggish
Virus checking will take time
Hacker attack would slow the system down
Less RAM available due to memory being allocated to data required for audio playback
Processor time used to playback music.

40. (a) (i) A method of storing audio data
A specification for storing audio data, for example: .wav
"Something which decides the way the sound file will be stored".

(ii) MP3 – music files
MIDI – small file size useful for transferring files over Internet.
MIDI can be recorded through keyboard and other MIDI instruments, files played back on a compatible instrument.
AU – used to be standard Internet audio format.
WAV – Microsoft format, supported by Windows browsers.
AIFF – developed by Apple, can support compression (AIFC).

(b) (i) GIF – common format, 256 colours, lossless compression so original file stored, small file size.

(ii) JPEG – millions of colours can be used, common format, small file size.
TIFF – any number of colours and options available.
BMP – Windows standard, uncompressed, complicated true colour pictures are stored so no decoder necessary.

Computing Higher 2005
Old Arrangements (cont.)

40. (b) (iii) Any two from:
Could include the text document which would be of better quality than a bit-mapped.
Could edit the text document before inclusion.
Text document smaller file size than scanned document.
No need to key in document.

(c) Identify key frame.
Changes to this frame are saved rather than all the data of successive frames.

(d) Any two descriptions from:
Transitions – how one frame is linked to the other (dissolve, wipe etc).
Audio – fade in/out, voice-overs etc.
Text – added to frames.
Timelines – frames can be deleted, added, moved etc.

(e) Capacity of DVD needed for digital video; CD-RW too small at 700Mb approx, need multiple CD-RWs.
Contents of CD-RW can be deleted whereas DVD is permanent.

Computing Higher
SQP 2005

Section I
1. (a) Pinpoints the address of the memory location to be accessed
(b) 0000 0011 0010 0000
(c) • Hold data to be processed.
• Hold the instruction being executed.
• Hold flags for the result of arithmetic or logic.

2. Larger range of characters i.e. 65 536.
Can cope with the characters of all languages.

3. (a) Any two from:
• It is removable and can be read directly by an appropriate computer system or printer.
• More than one flashcard could be carried allowing more photos on one trip.

(b) JPEG
Advantage – uses compression to reduce file size, supports millions of colours
Disadvantage – lossy compression means loss of detail
BMP
Advantage – no loss of detail, Windows standard, true colour pictures stored so no decoder required
Disadvantage – large file size, resolution dependent, cross platform incompatibility
GIF
Advantage – lossless compression, animation, transparency
Disadvantage – limited to 256 colours
TIFF
Advantage – any number of colours available
Disadvantage – tends to be a large file format

4. (a) Defragmentation

(b) Moves the component parts of a file to physically adjacent blocks.

(c) As a disc spins the next part of a file will be on the same track where possible, reducing the need to move read/write heads.

5. Program held in ROM that initiates the loading of the operating system.

6. Oversees whole project. Makes sure correct personnel are involved, time limits are not overrun, communication with the client, any other valid answer.

7. (a) Complete problem broken down into sub problems from top to bottom and each sub problem broken down further in order to solve whole problem.

(b) Easier to code, one to one mapping with the code, more manageable (e.g. program can be split more easily for a team of programmers).

8. Robust – can cope with any user input without failing.
Reliable – expected results are given every time the program is run.

9. (a) Repeating earlier stages in the SDP to make changes in order to produce correct results.

(b) Analysis – re-interviewing client to gather further information, going back to check current workplace etc.

10. (a) Array of Real

(b) Finding the minimum

11. (a) The High Level Language embedded within an application package.

(b) Complex tasks can be set up and initiated by a single key press or can save time going through endless menus (MACROS), user can customise the package to particular needs or features and functions which may not be given within the normal working of the package can be added.

Section II

12. (a) The Ruath should be chosen because ...
- It has a dual DVD/CD-RW drive. This would allow regular backup to CD-R(W)
- The Lynx has a floppy drive (too small for purpose) and a DVD-ROM (non-writable storage)
- Other suitable.

(b) • The performance will be enhanced/improved/made faster
- A cache will allow areas of main memory (RAM) to be held closer to the processor
- Addressing the cache uses shorter addresses which are manipulated faster reducing processing time.

(c) (i) • Clock speed may only be accurately used to compare processors of the same type
- A more powerful processor may achieve more in a shorter number of pulses
- other valid answers are possible.

- Clock speed is merely a measure of the frequency of timing pulses.

(ii) • MIPS – millions of instructions per second, actual number of machine instructions carried out in 1 second
- FLOPS – number of floating point operations per second, actual number of calculations done in 1 second
- benchmark testing – perform a series of standard tests designed to measure processor performance
- other valid answers may be possible – avoid general answers about measuring throughput.

13. (a) (i) peer-to-peer: Each station has the same status on the network. All stations can share files.
client-server: Some stations are clients some are servers. Only servers can share resources.

(ii) All resources can be installed on a fileserver making classroom management easier.
Files on server can be given appropriate access attributes to prevent accidental erasure of teaching materials.

(b) print server: to receive, store and prioritise print jobs from stations and print them on a shared printer.
web server: to store web pages and send them to stations on request.
mail server: to receive and store e-mail messages and forward them to their destinations.

(c) • file virus: attaches to the code of a program. It is run when the program is executed.
- boot sector virus: infects startup files, boot files, of the OS and is executed at startup time.
- macro virus: a virus in the shape of a macro. It attaches itself to a document and runs when the document is opened. It often copies itself to the macro library as a step towards copying itself to other files.

(d) • It doesn't have anti-virus software
- Used by many people who use external storage devices to transfer work from home to office.
- Virus writers target specific applications and operating systems
- Using software with known security flaws.

14. • Set up the Address Bus
- Activate the Read line on the Control Bus
- Memory accesses the relevant location and places contents on Data Bus
- Decode and Execute instruction.

15. (a) (i) Multimedia authoring package (or database)

(ii) Reason must include objects (different types of data, text/sound/graphic) and operations (searching/sorting/playing sound/etc).

(b) • 200 x 200 = 40000 pixels
- each pixel uses 4 bytes of memory
- 40000 x 4 = 160000 bytes
- 160000 / 1024 = 156.25 Kb

(c) Array of Strings

(d) • set found to 0
- for each member of the array
- if target = array(current) then set found = current
- end loop
- display found

Computing Higher
SQP 2005 (cont.)

16. (*a*) Through using the same variable name in several parts of the program there is a chance of overwriting a value accidentally.

    (*b*)   (i) Call by reference: The actual variable is passed into subroutine where it may be updated and the new value passed out. Call by value: The current value is passed into the subroutine, any changes made do not affect the rest of the program.

         (ii) Counters and name are by value as they should not be altered by the check. Win is by reference as it must be altered if the game is to end.

17. (*a*) • The formal specification is a legal contract.
       • Gives a clear and unambiguous statement of what the required software has to do.
       • Defines boundaries of the problem.

    (*b*) • Faster implementation by using pre-written code
       • Code is pre-tested
       • Shorter design time
       • Code is already documented.

    (*c*) Interpreter – Used during the writing of the software
       • May give better identification of location of error
       • Ability to test code despite presence of errors in code
       • Any other valid reason.

       Compiler - Used after the software has been completed
       • Produces object code for specific chipset therefore no need for subsequent translations
       • Object code runs without translator being present
       • Any other valid reason

    (*d*)   (i) Employee Code: DorwaG1999
         (ii) IF length(Surname$) > 4 THEN
             Set stem to first five characters of surname
           Else
             Set stem to surname
           End if
           Set initial to first character of firstname
           Set employee code to stem + initial + year

    (*e*)   (i) Adapts software to new environment. Example of new OS/printer/etc. acceptable.
         (ii) Adaptive is the responsibility of the client as it goes beyond original specification.

Section III – Artificial Intelligence

18. (a) Yes   Language constantly evolves and the ability to learn would suggest intelligence.
           Language is ambiguous and the ability to deal with such ambiguity demonstrates intelligence.
           Other possible answers.

        No   Only emulates or mimics intelligent behaviour.
           It is only a success in one narrow facet of intelligence.

    (*b*) (i) Human communicates with other human and a computer.
           If the subject cannot distinguish between them the test has been successfully overcome.

        (ii) Only a test of imitation of human discussion which is a very limited view of intelligence.
           If you cannot agree a definition of intelligence then you cannot agree a test for its existence.
           Other possible answers.

    (*c*) Ambiguity – the man hit the boy with the stick. Changing nature of language –e.g. fax, text etc. Same word having different meanings e.g. invalid.

    (*d*) No formal syntax for a query makes application available to non-expert users.

    (*e*) (i) Less likely to suffer loss of fridge contents due to a fault.
        (ii) Automatic call out for imminent faults giving repeat work for maintenance.
      (iii) Reorder food by swiping bar code, frequency chips.
           Sell by dates could be detected by fridge and displayed.
           View contents using picture messaging.

19. (a) No   Car features are regularly upgraded giving constantly changing knowledge base.
           Too many different types of cars making domain too large.
           Other possible answers.

        Yes   Domain is not too large – the number of different types of cars is easily implemented on modern computers.
           Most cars have similar features allowing the easy creation of rules.
           Other possible answers.

19. (b) (i) Expert System consists of KB –facts and rules
Inference engine – uses pattern matching to match query to facts and rules
User interface – provides interface through which to present dialogue boxes and questions and to provide solutions.
Expert system shell has empty or no KB.

(ii) Greater ability to customize HCI with procedural.
Greater access to mathematical functions, range of data types.

(c) Explanation increases user confidence.
Explanation will aid testing.

20. (a) (i) semantic net
(ii) analysis – The domain of the problem has been specified (narrowed) and understood correctly.
design – it represents the solution in a suitable design notation.
(iii) no need to consider syntax of KRL, graphical representation is easier to understand
aids coding by defining relationships of nodes to each other
allows easy creation of rules using paths from node to node

(b)

21. (a) Y= four_right_angles
Y= two_pair_parallel_sides
Y=opposite_angles_equal
Y= four_sides

(b) Matches at 8 Output Y=four_right_angles
Matches at 9, X becomes rectangle, sub-goal kind_of(rectangle,Z)
Matches at 3, Z becomes parallelogram, sub-goal has(parallelogram,Y)
Matches at 6,Output Y = two_pair_parallel_sides;
Matches at 7 Output Y = opposite_angles_equal;

(c) (i) no
(ii) is_a(trapezium, quadrilateral) results in yes, therefore the not means this is negated to a no.

(d) (i) Nodes adopt the properties of which they are a descendant.
(ii) Reduces the need for explicitly stating additional facts to establish the properties of a node.

22. (a) Depth-first requires less memory.
Depth-first won't always find the shortest solution.

(b) (i) Use an evaluation function to score a node and move to the best score available from that node. (Description of hill climbing).
(ii) Narrows the search space.
Reduces the search time.

(c) The number of possible nodes grows extremely quickly.
Becomes unmanageable in all but the simplest of problems.

Section III – Computer Networking

23. (a) • **Start**
<html>
Tag contains the entire document and identifies the page as valid HTML.
• **Header**
<head> ...</head>
Provides information to users and search engines.
• **Body**
<body> ... </body>
Contains the documents content.
• **Title**
<title> ... </title>
the same name given to the web page; the <title> element is located in the <head> element and is displayed in the browser window title bar, e.g. <head><title>Specimen Paper</title></head>.
• **Style**
<style> ... </style>
incorporates an internal style sheet; located in the <head> element.
• **Font Size**
<font> ... </font>
changes the font size and colour, e.g. <font size=5 color='purple' face="Times New Roman"> ... </font>.
• **Alignment**
<div> ... </div>
The division element is used to add structure to a block of text, e.g. <div align="right">.

(b) In both, <big>, <small> are used to produce a larger/smaller font.
Larger choices available in HTML such as <font size=5> to give one of the 7 sizes.

(c) Confusion with hyperlinks.

Computing Higher
SQP 2005 (cont.)

23. (*d*)   (i) "tapping" now applies to emails and mobile phone networks
investigations / surveillance regulated.

     (ii) Specific examples for and against are acceptable eg benefit fraud, CCTV activity, health and safety compliance with explanations. Candidates must make clear the "for" or "against".
or
Offence for communications to be intercepted without lawful authority {for} More organizations will be eligible to "tap" which means personal data harder to safeguard. For example: www.spelthorne.gov.uk/web/council/committees.

24. (*a*)   (i) Carrier sense multiple access with collision detection.

     (ii) A transmission may constantly collide with another when launched onto the network. Message will be resent after a random interval until it goes without collision. User may see this as slow transmission.

  (*b*)   (i) Data split into packets
Packets are individually routed
Packets are re-assembled in correct sequence once all received.

     (ii) improves communications when network is busy/running to capacity.

  (*c*)   (i) A single bit is added to the binary string to make the string have an odd number of '1s'. On receipt of data, the parity bit is checked, if check and actual agree transmission is assumed correct, if not error is reported.

     (ii) Double errors cancel each other out so error would not be spotted.
e.g. if 1110011 with odd parity bit 0 is received as 1101011 parity check will not fail since the reversal of the 3rd and 4th bits leaves parity bit unchanged.

  (*d*)   (i) Calculation performed on packet or block of data
Data and result of calculation transmitted
Receiving computer redoes calculation and accepts data or requests re-transmission.

     (ii) Speed decreases because of calculations needed at each end of transmission.
Accuracy of data increases because errors are discovered.

25. (*a*) DoS attacks disable a computer by bombarding it with a high volume of information requests in a short time, causing it to crash or become so overwhelmed that it grinds to a halt.

25. (*b*) Will prevent unauthorized users accessing the LAN
Filters data as it travels from Internet to LAN (packet filtering)
IP masquerading hides individual computers to the Internet so will reduce chance of a hit
Close/monitor ports.

26. (*a*) Data Link Layer

  (*b*) Transport Layer

  (*c*) The first octet is used to identify the network
The last three octets are used to identify the individual machine.

  (*d*)   (i) Class A is used for large networks and offers 224-2 useable IP addresses which is too big for the school network.

     (ii) Class C uses 8 bits for local addressing, this gives 254 useable IP addresses which is sufficient for the school.

  (*e*)   (i) World wide customer base rather than local/larger customer base
Catalogue up-to-date
Catalogue easy to change
Little/no paperwork/no salesman involved in collecting orders.

     (ii) Some companies, particularly small ones, do not comply with the laws relating to ecommerce
Security of data transfer, e.g. credit card numbers
Problems generally associated with mail order e.g. returns policy, delivery time, unable to see goods
Possibility of bogus company.

     (iii) Comply with Distance Selling Regulations
Include a privacy statement
Register with Information Commission
Operate a secure site
Payments linked to secure payment process, e.g. "PayPal".

Section III – Multimedia Technology

27. (*a*) Digital camera (or digital video camera with snap shot facility)
– The camera has a bank of Charge Coupled Devices (CCD) which it uses to capture an image digitally and store it onto a miniature disk or RAM in the camera itself. The original image is therefore captured as a stream of pixel data and then the camera or memory card can be connected directly to the computer for input.
Scanner
– A hard copy of the graphic is scanned. Light is reflected onto light sensitive diodes that translate the light into a voltage. An A to D converter translates each voltage into a digital pixel and this information is transferred to a software application which the data can be read from.

27. (b) (i) JPEG uses 24 bit colour (16 million) and GIF only uses 8 bit (256).

(ii) Colours which are not represented in the palette are displayed using a mix of pixels which are contained within the palette. This means that the missing colours can be represented.

(c) (i) Non-interlaced – each line of the image is drawn one after the other
Interlaced – every alternate line or bit (fuzzy to sharp) is drawn and then the rest after.

(ii) With interlaced the user can see the graphic build up and decide whether they want to view it before the full image is complete.

(d) $8 \times 640 \times 480$ bits
$= 1 \times 640 \times 480$ bytes
$= 307\,200$ bytes$/1024 = 300$ Kb

28. (a) Texture – mapping of flat image onto the cylinder
Rotate – cylinder has been rotated so that it has a different position.

(b) (i) Sphere {
Radius 1·0 (any number)
}
or description, e.g. name cylinder has to be changed to sphere and the correct dimensions given

(ii) Sharing 3D images over the Internet, platform independent, browser plug-ins can be used to view images, files can be created using a simple text editor.

(iii) When a browser reads a file the first line will help the browser determine what to use to display the file.

(c) (i) Files can be compressed and saved as smaller file sizes therefore less intensive on memory and storage requirements, decompressing for playback so files can be viewed, edited etc.

(ii) Increased bandwidth allowing the transmission of large data files, increasing number of client stations allowing accessibility to Internet etc.

(d) Multimedia content can be split up into separate parts for sound, video etc.

29. (a) (i) MPEG – lossy compression used (1 mark), only one full frame is stored in sets of 8 to 24 frames.

(ii) AVI – no compression so files are limited to 320×240 resolution and 30 fps, not adequate for full screen display, high backing storage and RAM requirements.

(b) Lower frame rate, reduce to 256 colours, use only a portion of the screen to display video (e.g. half screen size only needs half storage space).

29. (c) File size = resolution × frame rate × recording time × colour bit depth
File size = $800 \times 600 \times 25 \times 4 \times 3$ bytes
$= 144000000$ bytes
$= 137\cdot329$ Mb

(d) (i) CCD – collects and processes light coming in from the lens and converts it into an electrical signal.

(ii) DSP – adjusts signal for the optimum contrast and compresses data

(iii) Light is split into three primary colours (RGB) and each is fed into a different chip. This results in excellent colour and image quality.

(e) Wipe – screen divided into two sections by a line, 100% visible on one side. As line moves screen two appears
Dissolve – fade in and fade out at same time
Fade in – screen gradually lightens
Fade out – screen gradually darkens.

30. (a) Allows connection of input device (microphone), analogue to digital conversion, provides compression.

(b) No header used, PCM used to information convert from A to D signals, file's contents just a string of numeric data.

(c) MP3 – this format uses compression which does not save sounds that are drowned out by other noises, cannot be heard by the human ear etc and hence files sizes are smaller.
WAV – contain numeric samples of the actual sound that was recorded. The recorded sound can be sampled at various rates and the samples can be recorded as values of 8-bits or 16-bits in size.
RIFF – these files contain headers with textual information about the sound stored within the file.

(d) File size = Frequency × time × bit resolution × no. of channels
Fs = $44100 \times 120 \times 16 \times 2 = 169344000$ bits
Fs = $20\cdot187$ Mb

Computing Higher 2005
New Arrangements

Section I

1. (a) Area of memory in receiving device/interface/ peripheral.

   (b) Used to temporarily store data (in transit) between cpu and printer (thereby freeing the cpu to get on with other tasks).

2. (i) exponent

   (ii) mantissa

3. • Each pixel is represented by a (binary) number/bit
   • Stored as an array of pixels / grid of dots (must give idea of collection of pixels).

4. • Locate parts of files around disk (file is split up)
   • Re-order these
   • Into physically adjacent blocks / contiguous allocation of blocks
   • Thereby speeding up loading of files/file access/ gather free space at end of disc.

5. Web, multimedia(CD), application, mail, communication, proxy.

6. (a) 110000001

   (b) 10101010

7. Network Interface card (NIC)

8. gif, jpeg, tiff, bmp, png / any other valid answer.

9. Fewer fetches required to main memory as more data is cached.
   Pre fetching of more instructions

10. Document detailing the exact problem which the client would like a solution to
    Legal binding contract between parties
    Details (*fully* describes) the task that the system will perform.

11. Interview – question employees on current methods
    Observation – go into work place and study current practice, taking notes
    Study documentation – examine input and output which is required
    Questionnaire – generate information from many employees by issuing questionnaire.

12. Adaptive maintenance: the actual function of the software does not need to be changed; it just needs to be altered to accept input from a different source.

13. (a) pseudocode: written design uses English terms (to describe structures of program).

    (b) flowchart: graphical representation indicating flow of data and control structures
    structure chart or diagram: graphical representation indicating modular structure and hierarchy used.

14. global variable

15. String array, array of strings/char, array of records

16. Pre-tested so no need to go through exhaustive testing
    Pre-written so no need to write the code
    The code should be error free and should work correctly.

17. Procedural has data types, control structures etc which can be used.
    Modular/use of procedures/functions.

Section II

18. (a) Bitmapped
    - allows individual pixels to be edited **or** all digital photographs are bitmapped.

    (b) $4 \times 6 \times 800 \times 800 \times 16$ bits = 245760000 bits
    / 8 = bytes
    / 1024 = kb
    / 1024 = 29·3 Mb

    (c) Contents of flash card can be easily edited
    Flash card has higher capacity than CD-R (currently 1 Gb in most high street outlets)
    Flash card can be read by printer
    Flash card doesn't need computer to write to it (as CD does)
    CD-R disks are cheaper to buy
    CD-R cannot be changed once written
    Portability with suitable comparison.

    (d) Resolution – high quality photographs required
    Bit-depth – real life (true) colour required in photographs
    Print speed – fast to meet demand of many customers
    Different paper sizes – customers may require varying sizes of photographs
    Buffer size – larger buffer to free up the CPU when printing many/large photos.

19. (a) $2^{32} \times 24$ bits = 12Gb

    (b) Data format conversion – changing one data format used by one device into a suitable form for another device, e.g. analogue to digital, serial to parallel.
    Handling of status signals – signals used to show if a device is ready to send/receive data eg status signal on a printer can show that it is out of paper.

19. (c) (i) MIPS, FLOPS (MFlops), Application based tests
    (ii) MIPS – measures how many millions of instructions are processed in a second.
    FLOPS (MFLOPS) - measures how many floating point instructions processed in a second.
    Application based tests / benchmarking – measures certain criteria defined by the Application based test (applies a standard set of tasks).

(d) Address bus is set up with the address to be written to
Data bus is set up with data to be written
Write line (on control bus) is activated.
Place data in appropriate memory location.

20. (a) Not enough memory
Not enough backing storage
OS compatibility
Processor does not contain necessary functions to run package
Graphics card does not contain necessary functions to run package
Plug ins required

(b) The object could be
    - filled with a colour/pattern
    - line pattern/colour could be altered
    - line width could be changed
    - scaled/resized
    - rotated.

(c) Protect other processes
Check there is enough free memory
Select the area of memory to place the process.

(d) Inclusion of copyright images on a web page
Transfer of music files
Run software on 2 or more computers without correct licence.

(e) checksum, virus signature, heuristic detection, memory resident monitoring.

21. (a) (i) Actual client has an opportunity to ensure that software meets requirements.
    Bank can comment on program's operation.
    (ii) Comments made by client can allow changes to be made
    Cuts down on (corrective) maintenance later
    Monitoring the performance of the team.

(b) (i) The program produces correct results every time it is run
    or
    The program does not stop when executed due to design faults.
    (ii) Testing- where all levels of test data is used with all levels of possible users
    Each stage within the SDP is thoroughly checked and compared with software specification
    Module Testing, Systematic Testing, Comprehensive Testing.

21. (c)
```
Max= 1
For Page=2 to total number of pages
 If hits(page) > hits(max) then
        Max= page
 Endif
End for
```

(d) Not enough bandwidth is made available.

22. (a) Program does not crash and/or stop due to unexpected input.

(b) (i) Parameter passed is the actual variable itself (or the address of same), any changes to the parameter persist beyond the call.
    (ii) current value of variable is passed in, any changes do not affect the original value.
    (iii) Changes to the value do not effect the original variable, preventing unforeseen changes / preserving the original value for later use in the program.

23. (a) Allows user to customise package/menus for own needs
Allows macros to be created
Can be set up to enable complex commands to be carried out easily
Manipulation of data at a low level

(b) (i) Declarative – where a knowledge base of facts and rules is set up and can be queried
    Event driven – where objects such as buttons trigger the execution of code.
    (ii) Declarative – searches can be carried out through queries, without additional coding
    Event driven – could be set up for easy data entry where data operator just clicked on buttons to enter new records etc.

(c) (i) As an interpreter translates line by line, coding errors can be pinpointed and dealt with quickly.
    Able to run partial code (or code with errors in it).
    Able to identify syntax errors as they are typed.
    (ii) Using an interpreter, the loop would need to be translated every time the loop was executed. The interpreter would be resident in RAM during translation/ execution and every time the code was executed the loop would need to be translated every time (300), thus taking up processor time.

Computing Higher 2005
New Arrangements (cont.)

Section III – Artificial Intelligence

24. (a)   (i) X=neptune
      (ii) X= saturn Y=titan

   (b)   10 Sub Goal orbits(titan Y)
       8   Y = Saturn
       (Return solution Y = Saturn)

       11 Sub Goal orbits(titan Z)
       8   Z= Saturn

       11 2nd Sub Goal satellite(saturn Y)
       10 Sub Goal orbits(saturn Y)
       7   Y=the_sun
       (Return solution Y=the_sun)

   (c)   moon_of(X Y):- orbits (X Y),
                              planet(Y).

   (d) Huge number of known stars leading to coding of massive number of facts.
Large number of objects involved in orbiting the stars leading to coding of massive number of facts.
Difficulties in agreeing the definitions of objects leading to difficulty in coding rules for different definitions.

25. (a) Inference engine – pattern matches the query against the knowledge base
or
Chooses suitable rules to solve the query
Determines the question that the user is asked next.

   (b)   (i) The user can be held responsible
The expert system is to be treated as reference like a book.
      (ii) Unlike a human might generate no advice on given input.
Lack of common sense.
Have to update system regularly
Lack of imagination using unexpected input.
Inability to extrapolate from similar input with even one situation not programmed.
Narrow domain of knowledge and therefore advice.
Any other reasonable answer.
Variability of laws dependant on country.

   (c) Against – need to code the search methods/inference engine/coding of user interface.

   (d) Consistency of response, multi-access, 24/7 access, advice from many experts.

26. (a)   (i) Ability of a computer system to break down human language into its component parts, parse for syntax, derive meaning from human language.
      (ii) Expanding/evolving nature of human language, e.g. to text someone, surf the web etc.
Ambiguity in meaning of sentences, e.g. The man hit the boy with the stick.
Same word can have different meanings, e.g. building is a verb and noun (do not accept to/two/too etc as these are spoken word problems).

   (b) Could search for phrases based on the same meaning.
So phrases such as "rule out pneumonia" would not be reported.

   (c) Faster clock speeds allowing searching of the database to be completed quickly. More memory allowing more data to be held for analysis/parsing of sentences.

27. (a)   (i) XPFBY
      (ii) XPBYF

   (b) Depth-first since only the current path need be stored.

   (c) • Given several different starting paths from any given node.
• They could be evaluated independently.
• Using different processors giving faster response times.

   (d) • Human carries out a navigation for questioner
• Machine carries out same navigation
• Lack of ability of questioner to determine difference between two above.

28. (a) Finite and known set of quantifiable inputs. Access to large amount of existing data with output values for training.
Will be able to learn as the market changes.

   (b)   (i) Made up of layers of neurons with a set of input values each with its own weightings.
A calculation is performed on the input values which if it exceeds a threshold the neuron "fires".
      (ii) Iterative process
Using the existing and known criteria to input to a neuron and compare output to expected, weightings are adjusted allowing it to fire to produce correct output.

Section III – Computer Networking

29. (*a*) Advantage: security. Disadvantage: cost.

 (*b*) (i) • Data – addresses size of packet, means of addressing packet, preventing two nodes transmitting at same time (link, error and flow control).
   • Network – routes packets from one network to another (routing, switching and flow control over a network).
  (ii) • (Bridge), hubs, switches operates at the Data link layer.
   • router operates at the Network layer.

 (*c*) • Ensure compatibility of hardware and software around world.
  • Allow hardware and software from different manufacturers to be interconnected.

 (*d*) (i) Media Access Control
  (ii) Each device has a unique identifier (to prevent addressing errors).
  (iii) 24 bit address => 2^{24} or 16,777,216 million addresses.

30. (*a*) (i) • Each machine has a wireless network card (transmitter /receiver (radio/ infrared/ etc)).
   • Hub/switch receives and rebroadcasts signals from PCs **or**
   • Signals are passed between the machines.
  (ii) • No physical cables to lay/trip over
   • Flexibility of being able to move around
   • Physical structure of building presents no obstacles.

 (*b*) (i) It uniquely identifies a machine/device on the network.
  (ii) • IP address unique to machine and web address unique to site.
   • DNS keeps record of unique web address and matches to list of ISP's **or**
   • domain name resolution matches the IP address to the URL.

 (*c*) (i) • Data split into packets
   • Packets given destination address and sent
   • Each packet follows own route to destination
   • Packets reassembled into original order.
  (ii) Name a suitable protocol (http, FTP).

 (*d*) (i) $(112 \times 8)/15 = 59{\cdot}73$ seconds (or 1 minute).
  (ii) • bad packets needing re-sent/collisions of data
   • rest of message frame takes up space and hence bandwidth
   • another part of the network between host and students may be slower connection etc.
   • sharing bandwidth
   • integrity checks on file.

31. (*a*) Possible answers include:
  • faster or more reliable network cabling or other hardware (switches etc).
  • better networking software, easier to install and/or configure
  • greater standardisation of hardware/software through protocols or data standards
  • any other acceptable answer.

 (*b*) (i) Need for strategy: data loss through corruption, etc.
  (ii) Valid strategy involving regular (incremental/differential/full) backups taken **or** Backup held elsewhere. Use of large volume tape drive, or other suitable (DVD-R, DVD-RW, not just DVD) together with software to perform backups overnight, or other suitable answer.

 (*c*) • Multiple messages sent to the email server by attacker
  • Server cannot handle volume (thousands/millions are sent) therefore runs out of disk space.

 (*d*) Description of style or font size or alignment Poor description (includes forgetting the "/" close tags) of 2 tags.

 (*e*) Meta-search – transmits search to various search engines and their databases are searched. Spider – works through individual web pages and their links.

 (*f*) (i) Have a wider audience to advertise to, no need to pay retail staff or rent shop space etc, can be accessed 24/7 etc.
  (ii) Description of credit or debit card fraud or any other valid problem (returns, suitability of goods, phishing etc).
  (iii) Provide a secure socket layer, no order completion unless full details are accepted from customer, ISP or domain based address to be provided by customer, use of virtual on-line checking etc, encryption, digital certificates.

32. (*a*) Circuit-switching is where a circuit is established between sender and receiver prior to transmission and is maintained throughout transmission (leased lines etc.).

 (*b*) • The actual transfer is faster as no addressing information transmitted
  • Packets do not need to be re-assembled by the receiver.

Computing Higher 2005
New Arrangements (cont.)

Section III – Multimedia Technology

33. (a) (i) Storyboard
      (ii) • Shows links between screens, e.g. timings, transitions
         • Gives content of screens, e.g. placement of items, actual content
         • Shows common features, e.g. backgrounds, style sheets
         • Gives navigation links
         • Any other valid reason.

  (b) • Record the comments into his computer
      • using microphone, sound card (a to d converter) and digital audio software
      • Edit the audio clips using the digital audio software if needed
      • Import the clip into the presentation.

  (c) Sampling frequency × sound time × sampling depth × channels
      (11000 × 20 × 8 × 2)
      = 3 520 000 bits
      = 429·69 Kb

  (d) • Try all links to make sure they function as specified
      • Play all videos
      • Ask 'typical users' to beta test it.

34. (a) (i) 16 bit quality
         Ability to store waveform tables
         MIDI interface available
         Can mix or combine sounds
         increase number of channels
      (ii) 16 bit quality now gives CD quality audio
         Ability to store waveform tables allows simulation of instruments
         MIDI interface allows connection for input/output throughout eg keyboards.

  (b) allows hardware decoding of digital/sound/video files.

  (c) Both have dedicated co-processors to relieve main processor
      Both provide additional RAM
      Both do analogue to digital conversion.

  (d) Increase in storage capacity. Instead of recording only on the surface holographic technology records through the full depth of the medium.
      or
      Increase in speed of reading data. Holography allows a 'million' bits of data to be written and read in parallel with a single flash of light.

35. (a) • computer used for playback may not have same software that file was created with
      • standard file formats can be imported successfully into them/ease of data transfer with standard file formats.

  (b) RIFF describes the structure of a file using headers and chunks
      WAV files are RIFF files since they have the RIFF structure.

  (c) MP3 – music files (accept reference to hardware)
      AU – used to be standard Internet audio format
      AIFF – can support compression (AIFC)
      RAW (PCM) – High quality sampling, sample playback on embedded devices, etc.

  (d) (i) virtual reality markup/modelling language
      (ii) Animations and 3D imaging
      (iii) VRML describes a scene by attributes. Data is downloaded from the Internet; VRML viewers interpret the code then render it on the client computer thus saving download time.

36. (a) This frame identified as key frame (or description of key frame).
      Each subsequent frame is compared to this one. Only the changes are saved.

  (b) (i) • Picture quality reduced (detail removed)
         • Slow playback
         • reduction in frame rate.
      (ii) • Picture quality reduced: detail in the video may be removed by the compression technique used
         • Slow playback : Decompression takes time so playback may be affected
         • reduction in frame rate: frames rate reduced as part of compression.

  (c) (i) • Use a lossless compression technique
         • Play back on a computer with a faster processor.
      (ii) • Use a lossless compression technique: preserves all the original information.
         • Play back on a computer with a faster processor: compensate for time taken to perform decompression.

  (d) (i) Transfer speeds still relatively low 10m (limited) transfer range.
      (ii) • Bluetooth allows downloading by wireless connection, useful if out of doors since no need to carry separate wires as with USB
         • allows for distances up to about 10 metres so, e.g. could beam back to car, USB cable length restricts area of use
         • Many other devices, eg mobile phone, may have Bluetooth giving more interconnectivity and possibility of sending videos straight to a web page via his mobile phone.